BY THE EDITORS OF CONSUMER GUIDE®

THE COMPLETE BOOK OF
MARATHON
RUNNING

BEEKMAN HOUSE
NEW YORK

Contents

Manufactured in the United States of America
1 2 3 4 5 6 7 8 9 10

Published by:
Beekman House
A Division of Crown Publishers, Inc.
One Park Avenue
New York, New York 10016

Library of Congress Cataloging in Publication Data
Main entry under title:
Complete book of marathon running.
1. Marathon running. I. Consumer guide.
GV1065.C63   796.4'26   79-10369
ISBN 0-517-28845-1

Illustrations: Mike Muir
Shoe Diagram Illustration: Steven Boswick

Prologue

"Run 26 miles? You've got to be crazy!"

Crazy like a fox. Running a marathon is certainly not easy, but for those who've run one, the rewards have been great. Researchers have found that compared to non-exercisers, marathoners—

- have a lower percentage of fat;
- weigh less;
- have lower blood pressure;
- exhibit better heart-lung function;
- have lower cholesterol and triglyceride levels;
- have hearts that beat more efficiently;
- have a lower probability of blood clots forming in their arteries;
- have more efficient exercising muscles;
- enjoy better blood circulation;
- demonstrate better tolerance to stress;
- demonstrate a more positive frame of mind;
- suffer fewer heart attacks;
- live longer;
- have less hip osteoarthritis;
- show greater stamina;
- can afford to abuse their diets occasionally; and
- practice better overall health habits.

All of this is important and probably reason enough for you to try marathon running. And here is an endorsement you won't be able to ignore: The Occidental Life Insurance Company of North Carolina offers discounts up to 20 percent on its whole-life policies for those who exercise. To qualify, applicants must be at least 27 and less than 70 years old. They must sign a statement declaring that they have been jogging, swimming, or bicycling for at least 20 minutes, three times a week for the past year. As verification, they must take a medical examination. *Marathoners qualify automatically.* They do not have to pass a physical. All they need is documentation that they have completed a marathon. So marathon running can extend your life, make you healthier, prevent disease—and even save you money.

You may have another reason to run a marathon. Bob Glover (a contributor to this book) has called this race the "ultimate fitness challenge." If you have been running a half hour daily this year and been using CONSUMER GUIDE®'s *The Running Book* or our *Rating The Exercises,* you may be ready to extend yourself. The ultimate extension is 26 miles, 385 yards.

On the following pages we will show you how to run a marathon safely and effectively. This book is one of a kind. Its essays by experts explain in detail how new runners can complete a marathon. Charles T. Kuntzleman, the noted fitness and health authority, many other specialists in marathon running, and the editors of CONSUMER GUIDE® magazine, pooled their resources. The result is a book containing all you need to run your first successful marathon.

The Marathon Mystique

by Kevin Shyne

It is normally quiet on Sunday morning at Fort Wadsworth, a military installation on Staten Island. A few sentries stand guard over squat brick buildings on a hill near the Verrazano Bridge, the imposing link between Staten Island and Brooklyn.

But one Sunday last October, thousands of excited voices broke the usual quiet. Men with bullhorns blared out instructions. Helicopters chop-chopped over head. This was the start of the 1978 New York City Marathon.

The scene resembled a combination of a rock festival and a boot camp. One man dressed in a Superman costume claimed he was going to fly the distance. Others concentrated on pre-race sit-ups and push-ups. The 26th Army Band played patriotic tunes, while Red Cross trucks dispensed doughnuts and cups of coffee by the thousand.

The runners came from every state in the union and from 27 foreign countries. They were men, women and children of all ages, including doctors, lawyers, teachers, housewives, and students. There were blind runners led by sighted partners, and paraplegics competing in wheelchairs.

At 10:30 more than 12,000 people surged across the starting line on the Verrazano Bridge. The sight of the runners filling all six lanes of the world's largest suspension bridge was one of the most amazing sights of 1978.

Even more amazing is that this spectacle was not unique. Similar multitudes gathered for marathons in Chicago, Boston, Honolulu and San Diego. More than 170 marathons were held in 1978. Estimates of the total number of marathon runners ranged from 30,000 to 50,000.

At a time national leaders say America is running

out of energy, marathon mania is sweeping the country. No aspect of our culture seems immune.

Research scientists have studied the physiology of marathon runners and the health benefits of the sport. In 1976 the New York Academy of Science sponsored a symposium dealing exclusively with the marathon.

The news media have given marathons an unprecedented amount of coverage. ABC Sports televised live the entire 1976 Olympic marathon in Montreal. The 1977 Mayor Daley Marathon in Chicago was front-page news in city papers a week before and several days after the event.

American business has also responded to marathon mania. Shoe manufacturers have designed footwear especially for long distance races. A magazine just for marathoners started in 1978. Travel agencies even offer marathon vacations—charter trips to world famous marathons in Greece and Honolulu.

This surge of interest contrasts sharply with the relatively brief history of the marathon. Since the first marathon in 1896, it has largely been the sport of a handful of enthusiasts. Even in the mid-1960s the reknowned Boston Marathon attracted only a few hundred runners.

What explains this sudden interest in marathon running? It can be a terrible experience to run 26-plus miles. Why then this marathon mystique?

Part of the answer is the very word marathon. It calls to mind awesome challenges and heroic achievements. The event just would not be the same with a name like "a-bit-more-than-26-mile foot-race."

The word marathon refers to the legend of Pheidippides, a warrior at the Battle of Marathon, 490 B.C., who ran from the plains of Marathon to Athens to announce a stunning victory by the Athenian army over Persian invaders. Exhausted, Pheidippides staggered into the city, announced, "Rejoice, we conquer!" and dropped dead.

Most historians say that an anonymous writer invented the story of Pheidippides hundreds of years after the battle. After all, the Athenians could just as easily have sent a horseman as a runner — less poetic but more sensible.

The original account of the battle, written by Herodotus in the fifth century B.C., refers to a Pheidippides who belonged to a class of professional runner-messengers, the hemerodromi. Just before the battle, the Athenians dispatched Pheidippides to Sparta to ask for aid. He covered the 150 mile distance in two days. However, Herodotus does not say that Pheidippides—or any other messenger—ran to Athens after the battle.

Factual or not, the Pheidippides legend inspired a French scholar, Michel Breal, to devise the marathon in 1894. He put up a trophy for the winner of an Olympic long-distance race that would be named the marathon in honor of Pheidippides. Two years later the founders of the modern Olympics staged the race over the course the Greek hero might have taken centuries before.

Twenty-five runners started the first marathon, a 40-kilometer course from Marathon to the Olympic stadium in Athens. Villagers in towns along the way came out to cheer, and 70,000 spectators jammed the stadium.

The Greek spectactors were especially excited. The marathon was the last event of the Games, and no Greek had yet won a gold medal. The Greeks yearned for a victory.

The winner was Spiridon Loues, a slender 24-year-old Greek shepherd. Loues had fasted the day before the race and spent most of the evening before in prayer. His pre-race meal included an entire chicken.

The little shepherd won with a come-from-behind strategy. At about five miles, villagers in Pikarni told Loues he was far behind. He replied, "Do not worry. I will catch them and beat them all."

A French runner, Albin Lermusiaux, set a blistering early pace. But he began to tire at about 17 miles where the course went uphill. An Australian, Edwin Flack, passed Lermusiaux, as did Loues.

The Greek stepped along steadily and soon caught the Australian. They ran together for a mile, then Flack dropped back. He later collapsed and was carried to the stadium in an ambulance.

With less than two miles to go, Loues was nearly a mile ahead. He trotted into the stadium and crossed the finish line in 2:58.20.

His victory delighted the Greek spectactors. They showered Loues with applause and gifts. Some threw him jewelry and gold watches. A cobbler offered him free shoes for life. A tailor offered free clothing. Crown princes George and Constantine rushed from the royal box to the track, and jogged along with Loues for the last lap. The king saluted the new national hero with a wave of his hat.

Loues politely refused all the gifts, apparently to preserve his amateur status. However, he never again won a major race.

After this dramatic beginning, the marathon developed slowly. Road conditions were poor for running, and no one really knew how to train for the event.

For 40 years the marathon was not even a standard distance. It varied from 24 to 27 miles. In 1936 the Olympic Committee set the standard at 26 miles, 385 yards—the length of the 1908 Olympic marathon in London. The reason for the distance was simple. The London officials started the race in front of Windsor Castle so that the royal grandchildren could watch the start. From there it was exactly 26 miles, 385 yards to the finish line at the stadium.

After World War II the marathon gained much of its character from the personalities and achievements of several top runners. The first was Emil Zatopek, a good-natured Czechoslovakian soldier. In the 1952 Helsinki Olympics, Zatopek won the 5,000 meters, the 10,000 meters, and the marathon, an achievement unique in Olympic history.

Ironically, Zatopek had terrible form. His head wobbled. He panted and groaned loudly. One sportswriter commented, "He runs like a man who has just been stabbed in the heart."

Yet his bizarre form belied Zatopek's superb physical condition. His short, smooth stride never faltered. He ran at a killing speed, and his finishing kick was unbeatable.

Zatopek won with a time of 2:23.32, finishing his first marathon more than six minutes faster than the Olympic record. Amazingly, he recovered in minutes. By the time the next runner entered the stadium, Zatopek was munching on an apple and joking with friends. He later quipped to a reporter, "The marathon is a very boring race."

In 1960 Abebe Bikila, an Ethiopian palace guard who ran barefoot, won the Olympic marathon in Rome. Four years later, Bikila won again in Tokyo, becoming the only man to win two Olympic marathons. The Ethiopian wore shoes at Tokyo and covered the distance in the record-setting time of 2:12.11.

Abebe Bikila won the 1960 Olympic marathon running barefoot through the streets of Rome.

Few people knew Bikila well. He was detached and remote. Even in Ethiopia where he was a national hero, Bikila avoided publicity. He preferred to run, perform his duties as sports instructor in the Imperial Bodyguard of Emperor Haile Selassie, and spend time with his family.

Bikila's self-confidence was unshakable. He predicted his victories at Rome and Tokyo, and said he would win again at Mexico City in 1968. His chances seemed excellent. He would be accustomed to running at the mile-high elevation of Mexico City, since he trained in the mountains of Ethiopia. However, an ankle injury forced him to drop out of the race.

Bikila's running career came to a tragic end in 1969 when he was paralyzed from the waist down in an automobile accident. The Ethiopian government flew him to London for special treatments, but to no avail. Bikila spent the rest of his life in a wheelchair. He died in 1973 at age 46 of a brain hemorrhage and complications from his accident.

In 1972 Frank Shorter won the Olympic marathon in Munich, becoming the first American to win since Johnny Hayes in 1908. He placed second at the Montreal Olympic marathon in 1976. Although a foot injury has hindered him recently, Shorter is generally regarded as the king of marathoning.

Shorter's personality distinguishes him as much as his marathon record. Often interviewed, he talks about the marathon with intelligence and an ironic sense of humor. Yet he prefers not to talk about running too much. "It ruins the whole thing to take running too seriously," Shorter once remarked.

It is a beautiful sight to see Shorter run. His stride is light and precise. He seems to float along. Gifted with speed and endurance, Shorter excels in races from two miles up. He has covered three miles in 12:52, equivalent to a 5,000 meter run of 13:19, less than 12 seconds off the world's record.

In addition to physical talent, Shorter has a mental quality that makes him an especially strong competitor. It is a confidence and intensity that borders on cockiness. Kenny Moore, a world class marathoner and a writer for *Sports Illustrated,* noted, "There can be something hard in Shorter, a scornful quality, especially when he is out in front and applying pressure."

Shorter started running seriously late in his senior year at Yale in 1969. Told by the track coach he could make the Olympics and even win a gold medal, Shorter began working out twice a day. A month later he won the NCAA six mile championship. In three years he won the gold medal at Munich.

After Yale, Shorter went to medical school in New Mexico, but dropped out when it interfered with his training. He switched to law school at the University of Florida where he continued to train. Shorter now lives in Boulder, Colorado. He operates a running store and markets a line of Frank Shorter Running Gear.

In the mid-1970s Bill Rodgers emerged as America's newest marathon ace. He won the 1975 Boston Marathon in 2:09.55, breaking Frank Shorter's American record by 35 seconds. After a poor performance at Montreal, Rodgers began running better than ever. He won the New York City Marathon three times in a row starting in 1976. In 1978 he racked up a string of 19 consecutive wins, including the Boston and New York Marathons.

Rodgers has a friendly, fun-loving personality, seemingly unaffected by his recent running success. Amby Burfoot, winner of the 1968 Boston Marathon and his roommate at Wesleyan College, compared Rodgers to "a little puppy wagging his tail, hoping to please and waiting to play."

There is a story that Rodgers was out running when some kids started pelting him with green apples. Rodgers retaliated by ducking behind a tree and making faces at them.

Rodgers has had his ups and downs as a runner. He ran in high school and college, but didn't take the sport seriously. Senior year he stopped running altogether. He even started smoking.

After college, while doing alternate service in Boston as a conscientious objector, Rodgers took up running again. He increased his training while working at a state school for the retarded.

Rodgers' running career opened up in 1974. He placed 14th in the Boston Marathon and later took second in the National AAU 20 kilometer road race. The following spring he ran his record-setting Boston Marathon.

Rodgers likes to win and talks openly about his competitive drive. But he sees winning as a matter of running his best, not of beating the competition. At the 1976 New York City Marathon, Rodgers said he felt driven by a desire to run an excellent race. When Mayor Abe Beame crowned him with a victory wreath, Rodgers said simply, "It's over. Somebody had to win. It just happened to be me."

Rodgers lives in Melrose, Massachusetts, a Boston suburb. In 1975 he received a master's degree in special education. He taught emotionally disturbed children for two years, then opened a running store in Chestnut Hill, a few yards from the course of the Boston Marathon.

Not all the modern marathon giants have been men,

of course. In the past ten years women runners have pared nearly 45 minutes from the women's world record for the marathon.

Much of this improvement is due to increasing opportunities for women runners. Until recently the marathon was virtually a man's sport. Women were excluded by regulations based on uninformed notions that marathon running was too strenuous and unhealthy for them.

Undiscouraged, women marathoners in the late 1960s and early 1970s chipped away at official barriers to their participation. The Boston Marathon opened to women in 1972. The AAU held the first national marathon for women in 1974. In 1978 the 3rd International Women's Marathon in Atlanta attracted 184 runners from 12 countries. It also focused attention on the major remaining obstacle to women's participation—the reluctance of Olympic officials to establish an Olympic marathon for women.

One of the most remarkable of the modern women marathoners is Miki Gorman, a diminutive Californian who set a new women's world record at age 38. In 1973 she ran 2:46:36 at Culver City, California. In 1976 she won the women's division of the New York City Marathon with a time of 2:39:11, one of the fastest woman's times in history.

Gorman looks more like a tiny ballerina than a world class marathoner. She stands five feet and weighs only 89 pounds. Good-natured and friendly, she talks about running with the enthusiasm of a new jogger.

Gorman started running for her health. She joined a club in the spring of 1969, hoping exercise would relieve her chronic head and stomach aches. Gorman ran half a mile on her first day, then collapsed. But in six months it was clear she had a gift for distance running. She logged 589 miles in October, 85 of which she ran in the last day.

Gorman attributes much of her dogged endurance to her traditional upbringing. She was born in 1935 to a Japanese family living in China. Her father, a surgeon, controlled all her activities. He had planned to arrange her marriage, but died before he had a chance.

In 1963 she moved to the U.S. She spent a year on the East Coast, then moved to Los Angeles where she found a job as a secretary for a Japanese trading company. She met Mike Gorman, a stockbroker, and the two were married six months later.

She finished her first marathon in 1973 in 3:25. The same year she ran her record-setting marathon. Since then Miki Gorman has won the women's division of the 1974 and 1977 Boston Marathon and of the 1976 and 1977 New York City Marathon.

Along with top individuals, hordes of average runners helped create the marathon mystique of the 1970s. They changed its character from a grueling ordeal to a joyous participatory event.

Until recently few runners would bother to finish a marathon slower than 3:30. They trained hard and raced hard. But now the vast majority of runners finish between 4:30 and 5:30. Like Rocky in the movie, they run not to win, but to go the distance.

Not everyone is happy about the change. Huge numbers of runners have swamped marathon organizers. In 1977 organizers of San Diego's Mission Bay Marathon had to move the starting line, because the area used the year before was too small to accommodate all the runners.

More runners have also driven up the budgets of marathons. The numbers, portable lavatories, timing equipment and other expenses of the 1978 New York

City Marathon totalled approximately $350,000.

In addition, mass participation seems to threaten the simple, reflective quality long associated with marathon running. Runners at the start of a big marathon are packed together like sardines. Those at the back do not cross the starting line until five minutes after the gun fires. And woe to the poor soul who trips and falls.

Runners at the start of a big marathon are packed together like sardines.

Nevertheless, mass participation has meant that more people than ever before are experiencing the special joy of finishing a marathon. Many of them would never have considered starting ten years ago. Andy Anton, a 48-year-old Chicagoan who ran his first marathon a year after having a coronary by-pass operation, said, "I feel I've gotten a chance that others haven't had."

For runners like Anton, the marathon represents a special personal achievement. After finishing they are never quite the same again. Their stubborn persistence has paid off. They are marathoners.

Spectators sense this. That is why they cheer for all the marathon finishers, fast and slow alike. It is also why so many spectators now decide they would rather run than cheer.

Kevin Shyne is a writer whose articles have appeared in Runner's World *and* The Physician and Sports Medicine.

Making The Decision

by Bill Lundberg

"I'm going to run a marathon."

Good! You made the big decision. Skip this chapter and go on to the next chapter. You are ready.

For those of you still sitting on the fence, this chapter might help push you one way or the other. Maybe it will give you the nudge you need.

The decision to run a marathon is a highly personal one. One that nobody can make for you. Everyone may be asking you: "When are you going to run a marathon?" They may be telling you that you *should* run one. Talk is cheap. You know you are the one who has to log the hours and miles on the road. You are the one who has to face the icy blasts of winter and the stifling heat of summer. You are the one who will have dogs chasing you, cars trying to run you down, and people throwing things at you. You want to think this thing through. After all, you don't want to undertake a task and fail.

Let's put things in perspective. Take stock of where you're headed. Are you looking for a new challenge in your running? Do you get goosebumps watching Frank Shorter, Bill Rodgers, Gayle Barron, and Grete Waitz cross the finish line at a marathon? Do you wonder if you could cover 26-plus miles? Do you find that running has become a very big part of your life? Does the glamour of the "ultimate run" capture your imagination?

If you answered yes to two or more of these questions you're probably going to run a marathon some day.

Of course, the obvious question is: Why run a marathon? First, the great majority of you will decide to run the marathon because "it's there." You want to see if you can do it. It's like climbing the highest mountain, skiing the steepest mountain, or swimming the English Channel. The challenge is there and you want to do it. It's a thrill sport without having to jump out of an airplane, hang glide over a cliff, or race 200 mph in an automobile. It's also relatively inexpensive. Some people try to set records in marathon swimming, bicycling, and gliding, but at a great expense. Running a marathon, in contrast, is quite simple. It's not expensive—no large support systems are needed— just lots of miles and common sense.

Another neat thing about the marathon is that you don't have to set world records. Time is not the factor in the marathon; covering the distance is. That's the challenge. You want to see if you have the mind, spirit, and body to cover 26 miles, 385 yards. You are a champ if you are able to traverse the marathon distance.

Quite frankly, anyone with good health and a large amount of persistance can run a marathon. You simply have to be willing to take the appropriate amount of time and training to do it.

One of the biggest reasons for people wanting to run a marathon is that it gives you a chance to be with the big folks. All of us fantasize at one time or another that we'd like to engage in athletic contests with the champions of the world. We all have a little bit of George Plimpton in us. We want to enter the ring and see if we can go three rounds with Muhammad Ali. We wonder what it's like to catch Terry Bradshaw's game-winning touchdown pass in the Super Bowl. We dream of slam-dunking the basketball right past Jabbar's head. These are dreams that 99.44 percent of us never realize.

But with the marathon it's a different story. You can run with Shorter, Rodgers, and Barron. You may not be in their league, but you have been in the same race. You'll have run the same course, experienced the same weather conditions, heard the same crowd. You can say, "I ran with Rodgers or I ran in the Boston or New York City Marathon." So it's an ego trip, and a quite healthy one at that.

Further luster is added to the marathon in that each run is a new challenge. The course will be different, as will be the weather conditions. That way you can always run a personal best under various circumstances: snow, rain, sun, 30 degrees or 70 degrees.

One more thing. The marathon will give you physical and mental rewards. It is not destructive. It's ego building, healthy, and a chance to act out your fantasies.

Of course, there are some negative aspects of marathon running. And we're going to talk about these throughout the book. Quickly highlighted, the most negative part about marathon training is the extensive time commitment that you must give to running. An hour to an hour and a half each day is a good bit of your time. Secondly, you'll have to stick to a pretty rigid training schedule. Some of you may not like that lack of flexibility.

Another problem: though anyone reasonably healthy can complete a marathon, it doesn't follow that everyone should. You may not have the physical characteristics to run a marathon. You may be too fat, you may not enjoy running, or there may be some other extenuating circumstances. If that is the case, don't do it.

Finally, the marathon is a grueling race. It can drain you physically and mentally. Marathon running may be hazardous to your health if you don't follow the proper guidelines.

Despite these problems, if you should still decide to

run a marathon you need a game plan. One that will take you through the proper steps so that you will be successful. That's what this book is all about—a basic guide to marathon running.

Before we take you step-by-step to the promised land of marathoning, there are several factors you should consider.

Your goal is to complete a marathon; not to compete in one.

You are to run a marathon only if you want to; not because someone is there telling you to do so.

You should not enter a marathon with the intention of losing weight or getting into shape. You should only run a marathon after you have gotten back into shape and built a base of 20 miles or more a week for several months or more.

You are to follow the schedule in this book. But don't be a slave to it if social, physical, and mental distractions crop up. Learn to be flexible. There are plenty of other marathons to choose from. If you try to stick to a rigid training schedule and find your work schedule precludes it, you may have to pick a more appropriate time.

You should learn to listen to your body. If your training pace seems too difficult or you seem excessively tired after a run, back off. If you think a rest day is in order, take the day off. Roger Bannister, the first sub-four minute miler, took four days off three weeks before he broke the four minute mile barrier. He did this because the training was just too intense. He needed some time away from the track. If a top-flight runner such as Roger Bannister could relax, you certainly can.

You are not to run more than 20 miles when training. In this book we have plans to get you ready for a marathon. But these plans don't include runs longer than 20 miles in preparation for the marathon. You are still a novice at this idea of marathon running. You'll just have to trust the experts at CONSUMER GUIDE® magazine. The natural tendency is to want to run 26

You are the one who has to face the icy blasts of winter when training for a marathon.

miles to "see if you can do it." Don't try it. It can wipe you out for weeks. Stay at 20 miles or less. Going further can injure your marathon performance.

You are to make haste slowly. Do not think you can up your mileage by leaps and bounds. A 10 percent increase each week is plenty. More than that will wear you out and set you up for a host of physical and mental ailments.

You should not get caught in the trap of thinking that while running the marathon you must run all the way. Don't be such a purist. In fact, you may find that walking up the hills will be faster than running up them. Your goal is to cover 26 miles (not set a record—remember?).

You should recognize that the last six miles or so of the marathon will be a bear. You will hit "the wall." You'll hate yourself and your world. You'll wonder why you ever started this crazy idea in the first place. But remember, everyone, even the best, agonize. Running a marathon is no Sunday afternoon picnic. It's hard work. And one of the most important ways you can reduce that agony is to follow our guidelines.

You should also remember the collapse-point theory in marathoning. This theory says that your training mileage of the previous eight weeks sets the limit on how far you can hold a certain pace. The limit is about three times your daily run. So, if you're averaging six miles a day you expect to hit the wall or reach your collapse point 18 miles into the run. And when you hit this point your pace will be slowed considerably.

If you are still with us and have made the decision to run a marathon you should consider the following.

Step 1: SET A GOAL. Your overall goal has already been taken care of. You have a specific objective. You want to run a marathon. We think it's a good idea to record the date that you plan to run the marathon. Write it down on a sheet of paper. Once a week, take out the sheet of paper and look at it. You might want to write down your progress and what has happened over the last week.

Although you have a specific goal you do need to plan how you're going to reach that goal. The guidelines in this book should be helpful. Here, however, we want you to be specific. Write down how many minutes of running or miles you are going to do each week. Even if you write the same thing that we have recommended, indicate how much you are going to do, daily. Also write down some motivators you're going to use to help yourself continue.

Finally, write down what you're going to do today. Not tomorrow, but today. Indicate how long, at what time, and where you're going to run. Each morning as you get up do the same thing until you reach your goal of running a marathon.

Step 2: RECORD YOUR PROGRESS. Although this book outlines exactly the steps you should follow and you have written those steps down, a progress chart allows you to compare yourself with it. It tells you, and anyone else who looks at it, how well you're doing. You and they know how close you are getting to your goal. It gives you a feeling of accomplishment.

The chart doesn't have to be complicated. The simplest one is a calendar with information written in. Many people record their mileage on a map. Your regular running route may take you around the same section of your neighborhood every day. But you can mark off your distance on a map as though you were running cross country. By the end of the year you may find that you've run a distance equal to that between

New York and Des Moines, or between New York and Miami. The map helps in setting long-term goals, too. For instance, you can promise yourself that you'll run from Chicago to Philadephia this summer.

Step 3: MAKE A TIME COMMITMENT. Have you ever noticed how easily you slip into routines? Perhaps you always brush your teeth before, not after, you shower in the morning; always put your left, not your right, shoe on first; take the same route to work every day. And have you ever noticed how you tend to feel you've forgotten something important if anything should interfere with this strange ritual? You may find it easy to stay with a running program if you can allow it to become part of your daily routine—so much a part that you'll feel compelled to run despite your own excuses for skipping a day. If you can get yourself into the habit of running at a certain time every day, you accept it as part of your daily routine and not just something to do at odd moments.

Whatever you do, don't worry about taking the time. Your co-workers may take a two hour, three-martini lunch and think nothing of it. And they may cast a scornful eye at you as you go off to take your run at noon. But you're doing something positive for your body, and it will make you feel better, more productive, more alive.

Step 4: CHOOSE THE BEST TIME OF DAY. The best time of day depends on you. Some runners like to run early in the morning. Some even before daybreak. They seem to like the solitude available at that hour, when the streets are still empty of traffic and people. They can slowly get their minds and bodies going and do a little thinking in silence. And if they are running where they can see the horizon, they can savor the exhilarating sight of dawn.

If you do run before going to work, it's probably a good idea to nibble on something beforehand so your body has the fuel it needs for the run. There are really no ironclad rules, but something very light such as a piece of toast and a small glass of orange juice is best.

Some people skip lunch and use that time to run. It gets them out of the office or house and into a refreshing midday break. Other runners wait until they have left their work, put their jobs behind them, and headed home. A run at this time provides a good transition for them, a time to work off some of the day's tensions so that they don't have to carry them into family life.

Late evening seems to appeal to some people as the best time. Unfortunately, there are some negative aspects of running late at night. First, when you put running in as the last thing on your agenda for the day, it often gets treated that way—last. You tend to put other things in place of it. You either forget it, "just don't have the time," or lack the energy to do it. Second, when you run late in the evening, you may find it difficult to sleep afterwards. So be cautious.

Step 5: THINK THE PART OF A MARATHON RUNNER. What happens in your head is almost as important as what happens to your body, because if you don't enjoy what you're doing you're going to find reasons for not doing it.

Read as much as you can about marathoning. Talk to other marathoners. Watch marathon races, if possible. Try to visualize what the race will be like for you.

Step 6: RUN WITH OTHERS. If you're married, your spouse ought to be at your side. A study conducted at the Heart Disease and Stroke Control Program bears this out. Men in an exercise program did one hour of physical activity three times a week for eight months. If a wife encouraged participation, the individual's attendance was good; if the wife was neutral or had negative feelings about the exercise, attendance was much poorer. Conclusion: the spouse's attitude was critical. If you can get your spouse to run with you—so much the better.

Running with a friend gives those so inclined the advantage of companionship and encouragement. These people will run more if they have someone to talk to and to keep them company.

In an investigation conducted at the University of Toronto, scientists reported a greater dropout rate for individual, rather than group, programs. Only 47 percent of those on an individual program were still active after 28 weeks, compared with 82 percent for those in group programs. If you feel your motivation may be weak, run with a partner or with several friends.

Running marathons has become a fascinating phenomenon in America. Don't run a marathon because everyone else is. Run one because you want to. The best motivation in the world is intrinsic. If your head is ready, your legs will follow right along.

We warn you that training and the actual marathon run itself will not be easy. You'll need considerable self-discipline. You'll need some real stick-to-itiveness to accomplish what we're going to tell you to do in the next chapters. But the marathon is the true test of a runner. In the marathon you will find out what you're made of.

———————

Bill Lundberg is the U.S. steeplechase champion and an Olympic hopeful for 1980.

The Importance Of A Base

by Bob Glover

Thousands of runners each year are competing at the marathon distance. Thousands more annually witness such spectacular events as the New York City Marathon and the Boston Marathon and decide—"Next year I'm going to run the marathon!" The odyssey from marathon spectator to marathon finisher can be a very involved, dangerous process. But it can also be a very simple, successful process.

According to Richard Traum, "Anyone who honestly takes the time to train, to build the necessary base, can finish a marathon." Traum started as a raw beginner in one of my fitness programs in the summer of 1975 and went on to finish the 1976 and 1977 New York City Marathon. His 1977 time of 6 hours and 45 minutes is the fastest time ever recorded for an above the knee amputee. I have worked with many exceptional people—the blind, postcardiacs, 70-year-olds—who have successfully completed marathons. Almost anyone can run a marathon *if* they train for it properly by building a base of aerobic fitness and then progressively expanding that base to an appropriate level.

Perhaps one can best relate to proper marathon preparation by following the development of a typical runner. In this case, the example is Jack Shepherd, my co-author of *The Runner's Handbook.*

I first met Jack in December, 1975 when he was tested for entrance into one of my beginner fitness classes. He was in terrible shape with an abnormally high resting pulse and a borderline blood pressure reading. He claimed he got out of shape while writing *The Adams Chronicles.* I remember laughing about how one could possibly get so worn out by just sitting around writing. Later I would identify more closely with his problem. So Jack was the typical 39-year-old, sedentary, overstressed American who was a prime candidate for heart disease—certainly not marathoning. At first he couldn't run more than two laps of the gym. As a professional journalist he was more adept at banging away with his fingers at a typewriter or downing martinis for lunch than running and—ugh, sweating.

After ten weeks he had progressed to being able to run comfortably for twenty minutes. Within six months he was enjoyably running five miles three times a week. For the entire 1977 running year Jack averaged twenty miles a week and I felt he was ready for a marathon training program. He wasn't the slightest bit interested. But then something dramatic happened. He stood at the finish line of the 1978 Boston event and watched his first marathon. Suddenly another marathoner was born. The training program Jack used became the marathon build-up program in *The Runner's Handbook Training Diary* which *starts* at a base of twenty miles a week. Working from that base, Jack worked up to 50 to 60 miles a week and easily finished his first marathon in New York City in October 1978.

The saga of Jack Shepherd was a three year process. Dick Traum made the transition from sedentary businessman to marathoner in one and a half years. The average length of time for the many novice marathoners I have coached from their first running steps to the marathon finish line is two to three years. The range depends upon such factors as age, previous athletic experience, avoidance of injuries, etc. Starting from sedentary marathon watcher one should progress to marathon racer in seven steps.

Step 1: Make a commitment as is detailed in the preceding chapter.

Step 2: Become a runner—build to running twenty continuous minutes at least three times a week. This process, as detailed in this chapter, takes on the average six to twelve weeks.

Step 3: Become an intermediate runner—build to a base of twenty miles a week. This process takes, on the average, another four to eight weeks and is detailed in this chapter. One should then remain at this level for two months or longer.

Step 4: Become a racer. Experience a few races of four miles to a half-marathon before deciding to enter a marathon. You need to learn the racing and pacing process.

Step 5: Follow a three to six month build-up program from the twenty mile a week base, aimed towards that first marathon.

Step 6: Run a marathon. Experience it first without any time goals.

Step 7: Race a marathon. Training and experience can be combined to reach the goal of improving the marathon time.

A base is extremely important in any endeavor. Building a house starts with laying a proper foundation—otherwise the house can come toppling down. The same is true of marathoning. If you attempt a marathon without first building a proper foundation you risk the frustration of not finishing. Furthermore, you endanger your total physical and mental health. Your base should involve four concerns—

1. developing a trained cardiovascular system—aerobic work;

2. developing a trained musculo-skeletal system;

3. developing running experience; and

4. developing mental confidence.

When you exercise, your heart is forced to work harder in order to pump oxygen-enriched blood to the working muscles so that the desired work can take place. Exercise strengthens the cardiovascular system, making this progress a more efficient one. If you are a beginning runner you must slowly and progressively develop the efficiency of this system so that your heart isn't dangerously overtaxed. By building up a base of cardiovascular strength, you prepare the heart for the rigors of marathon training and marathon running. This base training should be aerobic work since marathon running is aerobic work. Thus all base training should be done at a pace so your heart rate stays within your safe training range for twenty to thirty consecutive minutes or more. At this level the heart can supply the working muscles with enough oxygen to meet the demand and not go into "oxygen debt." Base training, therefore, should be done at a pace at which you can comfortably talk and remain within your prescribed training heart rate range. The first marathon experience is a test of endurance, not speed. Thus anaerobic speed work is totally unnecessary as well as potentially dangerous for an inexperienced runner.

The process of slowly building a base also allows for your musculo-skeletal system to adjust to running progressions. Your foot hits the ground at three times the force of your body's weight when running. Thus the muscles, bones, and joints of the body absorb a tremendous amount of shock. A sudden switch from sedentary activity to marathon training can result in many injuries. Often your cardiovascular system can adjust to increases in training more steadily than the musculo-skeletal system. That is why I am very, very conservative in progressions made in runners' schedules in my programs.

It is also important for you to build a base of experience before getting into marathoning. Important lessons such as how to dress properly in varying weather conditions, how to pace yourself, etc., can really only be learned through personal trial. With experience and the triumph of progressive increases in performance come increased confidence. If you believe in yourself and know you have a proper base for marathon training, then success is merely several miles of patient training away.

How do you build a base? I have trained over 10,000 men and women of all sizes, shapes, and ages over the last seven years by using three methods. My techniques were based on knowledge I gained from my students. The students in a fitness program are actually the teacher. The goal of each method is to first build to a base of approximately twenty minutes of comfortable running at least three times per week and then expand that to a level of thirty minutes of comfortable running at least three times a week. From this level you can increase to a base of twenty miles a week.

Before describing how to reach the first level of this base preparation it is important to emphasize the three essential phases of a running program: warm-up, running, and cool-down. The exercise session should *always* start with a proper warm-up and end with a sufficient cool-down regimen.

The warm-up consists of three parts: relaxation, stretching, and the gradual build-up of the heart rate to the desired training range. At least fifteen minutes of relaxation and then stretching exercises are essential. Relaxation allows the body and mind to release tension and become prepared for the activity to follow. Slow, easy stretching, particularly for the hamstring and calf muscles and the Achilles tendon, are important in that they lengthen the muscles and tendons which can become tight otherwise. This process helps to prevent injuries from occurring. The beginner runner should then walk for five minutes to gradually build the body heat and heart rate up towards the training level.

The cool-down is simply the warm-up in reverse. At the conclusion of the run a five-minute walk will lower the heart rate towards the pre-exercise level and allow for blood to flow back from the extremities to prevent potential problems that could occur if one were to suddenly stop exercising. "Pooling of the blood" in the legs deprives the heart and brain of sufficient blood-flow. At least ten minutes of stretching and then relaxation exercises are necessary to prevent stiffness and to allow for a feeling of post-run calm. The pulse rate at the conclusion of the session should be within twenty beats of the pre-exercise pulse, or approximately below 100.

The primary technique I use for large masses of runners is my "Run-Easy Method," which is the basis of *The Runner's Handbook.* Simply, the runners are given a twenty minute work period during which they alternately run and walk. They run aerobically—at a conversational pace—until they feel they need to walk. They run within themselves, conservatively but progressively. When their lungs or legs yell at them to slow down, they walk briskly until they are ready to run again. As days and weeks go by they run more and walk less. Eventually they build up to a level where they can run for twenty continuous minutes comfortably. It took Jack Shepherd ten weeks to arrive at this point. His progression was very conservative, however, since he had been a hypertensive person and very sedentary. The normal time period for the beginner, building up to twenty continuous minutes, ranges from six to twelve weeks, depending upon such factors as age, weight, and previous athletic background. The runner should stay at this level for a few weeks before gradually moving up to thirty minutes per session.

A second method of training beginners is used in the Saturday morning running program that I direct for the New York Road Runners Club. Runners of all levels meet in Central Park for warm-ups and then are broken down into groups based on their running background. Beginners are led around the 1.7 mile loop of the reservoir. They are instructed to run at a conversational pace with others of a similar speed until they feel a need to walk. They then walk briskly until they are ready to run again. This type of progression should be followed at least three times a week. As weeks go by they run more and walk less until they reach that triumphant day when they can complete the entire loop running and smiling. They keep this pattern up for a few weeks and then start running two loops—once again taking periodic walk breaks until they can run the full time. Thus, you can set a distance of one and a half to two miles as a goal and gradually progress from run-walk to running. This system offers tangible evidence of improvement. You may then brag about running from your house to the store and back, etc.

Some runners need a more structured approach. A simple technique would be to run for half a block and then walk half a block, gradually increasing the running and decreasing the walking. Running guides such as telephone poles can also be used to help monitor progression.

I direct the national running class program for the Connecticut Mutual Life Insurance Company's "Run For Life" program which is based on the premise that many beginner runners need a set progressive program. The program began with a pilot twelve week class in New York City and is now being expanded across the country. It is based on the build-up program detailed in *The Runner's Handbook Training Diary.* Runners start with a program of one minute of running followed by two minutes of brisk walking over a period of twenty minutes. After eight weeks of set progressions of minutes running versus minutes walking they are able to run for twenty continuous minutes. After this level is reached, they move up to thirty minutes of running by the end of the twelve weeks. This type of enforced slow progression insures the runner that the body won't be overworked in the early stages of the program, but offers enough weekly challenges to promote improvement.

The average beginner runner will take eight weeks to build to a level of twenty minutes of running which should be done at least three times a week. That is the minimum of exercise needed to be physically fit. Twenty minutes of running is considered to be the prerequisite base for intermediate running. The intermediate gradually increases to at least five or six days of running a week for periods of at least thirty minutes. Assuming a pace of approximately ten minutes a mile, the runner who is covering thirty minutes a session, five times a week will be covering fifteen miles a week. The next step in base building would be to remain at this level for a few weeks and then gradually build to the twenty miles a week marathon base. The runner should stay at this level for a few weeks or months to allow the body to adjust to the demand. Ideally, you would progress from a sedentary state at a rate similiar to that shown in the following chart.

Building A Base

Length Of Run	Times Per Week	Minimum	Maximum
		(months)	
1. Build to			
20 minutes	3-5	2	3
2. 20 minutes	3-5	1	2
3. Build to			
30 minutes	5	1	2
4. 30 minutes	5	1	2
5. Increase to			
20 miles total	—	1	2
6. 20 miles total	—	1	12

Each of you will vary in your desire and ability to follow this build-up schedule. It is only a sample guide meant to emphasize the importance of slowly and gradually following a schedule of base development. Some of you may decide to stick to the bare fitness minimum of twenty minutes of running three times a week for years before catching the marathon bug, or perhaps before you are physically prepared. *Remember—not everyone has to run marathons, not everyone is made to run marathons.* In fact, the marathon *can* lead to a lower level of fitness with long layoffs—the recuperative periods caused by physical and mental injuries associated with marathon training and marathon racing. Some of you, especially those with previous athletic background, will be able to progress much faster than these conservative guidelines. Additionally, some of you have previously been doing some running and thus can start at an appropriate level along the progression schedule outlined.

In general, the average non-runner who sees his first marathon and exclaims, "Next year I'm going to run the marathon," needs a full year just to build a proper base for marathon training. Thus the man who approached me after the 1978 New York City Marathon who was running fifteen miles a week, could be ready for the 1979 event if he gradually builds toward that goal. His friend, however, who is completely sedentary, should consider the 1980 event a more logical goal.

A typical one year program builds from ground level to a solid base of twenty miles a week (according to the previous chart), and moves on to the progressions depicted in the following chart.

After you reach thirty minutes of running for five workouts a week, I usually switch you over to recording mileage instead of minutes. I do this since races are run based on mileage covered and thus it is easier to relate training mileage to racing mileage than training time to racing time. Many runners, however, record their workouts only by time. This is a personal preference to be determined by each of you. In this sample schedule I assumed that when you covered 3 miles in thirty minutes you were running at an average pace of ten minutes a mile. Three miles a day, five times a week gives you a total of fifteen miles.

A One Year Program

Week 1-8:	Build to 20 minutes of running, 3 days a week.
Week 9:	20 minutes, 3 days a week.
Week 10-11:	20 minutes, 4 days a week.
Week 12-16:	20 minutes, 5 days a week.
Week 17-18:	22 minutes, 5 days a week.
Week 19-20:	24 minutes, 5 days a week.
Week 21-23:	27 minutes, 5 days a week.
Week 24-28:	30 minutes (3 miles), 5 days a week. Total: 15 miles a week.
Week 29-30:	3 miles, 3 days a week; 4 miles, 2 days a week. Total: 17 miles a week.
Week 31:	3 miles, 3 days; 2 miles, 1 day; 4 miles, 2 days. Total: 19 miles.
Week 32:	3 miles, 3 days; 2 miles, 1 day; 4 miles, 1 day; 5 miles, 1 day. Total: 20 miles.
Week 33-52:	20 miles a week.

Up to week 31 in this sample the schedule included no more than five running days a week and then expanded to six days. Once again this is a matter of personal decision. I prefer allowing for at least one planned rest day a week for all of my runners until they become serious marathon racers.

The running schedule should follow a pattern allowing for variety and rest. Twenty miles a week shouldn't mean three miles a day, seven days a week, at the same pace and over the same course. (See chart below.)

Sample 20 Mi/Week Schedule

Mon.	Tues.	Wed.	Thurs.	Fri.	Sat.	Sun.
Off	3 miles	4 miles	3 miles	3 miles	2 miles	5 miles

In *The Runner's Handbook* I refer to the marathon as "The Ultimate Fitness Challenge." In my lectures I refer to those who wish to try their first marathon adventure as people approaching the lunatic fringe. You have to be a little crazy to want to run 26 miles, 385 yards. It is only glamorous after you cross the finish line. Before that, months of work and careful preparation are necessary. In the end, however, you will be just as proud of how you intelligently built a base for the cake—the taste of personal victory as you cross the finish line serves as your frosting.

Bob Glover is co-author of The Runner's Handbook.

The Preparation Plan

**by The Editors of
CONSUMER GUIDE® magazine**

Bob Glover has explained the importance of base mileage in running a marathon, a base that averages 20 miles a week over a one month to one year period of time. Once you have established this base and feel comfortable with it you are ready to up your mileage. You are ready to begin training for a marathon in earnest.

In this chapter we have provided a 12-level training program. Quite frankly, the 12 levels could be 12 weeks. Some of you, however, will find it necessary to spend two weeks at each of the levels described. It depends. Each person is different. Each one of you will progress at your own rate. The rate at which you progress depends upon your base mileage, general health and stamina, age, and previous athletic pursuits and endurance endeavors.

The aim of the CONSUMER GUIDE® magazine marathon plan is to condition your heart, lungs, muscles and bones to run 26-plus miles. It is also to prepare you mentally to run three hours or longer. Briefly summarized, in this marathon plan you will be taking yourself through twelve levels of conditioning, with progressive stages of conditioning at each level. The conditioning goals are met naturally and automatically as you progress through the program. The most important thing about it is that you advance easily and comfortably, in step with your own body's demands.

The program also makes the assumption that you will be running at your own target heart rate level, a level that is best for you.

In *The Running Book,* the Editors of CONSUMER GUIDE® magazine explained that everyone has what is called a "maximum heart rate," generally based on age and current physical condition. A person's maximum heart rate is the number of beats his heart

Your Target Heart Rate and Heart Rate Range

Maintaining your target heart rate is the key to the CONSUMER GUIDE® running program. Your maximum heart rate is the greatest number of beats per minute that your heart is capable of. During exercise, your heart rate should be approximately 75% of this maximum. To obtain the cardiovascular benefits of running—or of any other exercise—you maintain a heart rate between 70% and 85% of your maximum, for at least 15 and preferably for 20 minutes. If your heart rate is less than 70% of the maximum you will not improve your cardiovascular condition. If it exceeds 85% of your maximum, you are overdoing and should relax your pace.

Age	Your Maximum Heart Rate	Your Target Heart Rate (75% Of The Maximum)	Your Target Heart Rate Range (Between 70% And 85% Of The Maximum)
20	200 beats per min	150 beats per min	140 to 170 beats per min
25	195 beats per min	146 beats per min	137 to 166 beats per min
30	190 beats per min	142 beats per min	133 to 162 beats per min
35	185 beats per min	139 beats per min	130 to 157 beats per min
40	180 beats per min	135 beats per min	126 to 153 beats per min
45	175 beats per min	131 beats per min	123 to 149 beats per min
50	170 beats per min	127 beats per min	119 to 145 beats per min
55	165 beats per min	124 beats per min	116 to 140 beats per min
60	160 beats per min	120 beats per min	112 to 136 beats per min
65	155 beats per min	116 beats per min	109 to 132 beats per min
70	150 beats per min	112 beats per min	105 to 128 beats per min

makes per minute when his body is undergoing maximum exertion. Your maximum heart rate will generally be 220 beats per minute, minus your age. If you are 20 years old, your maximum heart rate will be 200. If you are 60, it will be 160. This formula is derived from the observation that for each year you live your heart loses about a beat a minute.

The "target heart rate," as it is called in cardiovascular exercise programs, is pegged at around 70 percent to 85 percent of your maximum heart rate. Everyone's heart and overall physiology is different, so the target heart rate of individuals is normally described as falling within a target heart rate range. The accompanying chart "Your Target Heart Rate and Heart Rate Range" gives the maximum heart rate, the target heart rate range, and the target heart rate for ages 20 through 70 in five year increments. You can calculate your own rates and range from this if your age falls between the ages listed.

Your target heart rate is your own built-in system which tells you if you are working too hard or not hard enough. Don't be a total slave to this target heart rate guide, however. If you find running at your target heart rate level to be much too difficult, slow down. If it seems as though you could be at a higher pulse rate and running comfortably, speed up. Your personal feelings are the most important indicator. The target heart rate zone simply gives you a ball park figure. Undoubtedly, most of you started running with the target heart rate concept as your guide. But this review may have been helpful. The "Three To Six Month Training Schedule" shows you how to progress from Level 1 to Level 12. The discussion following the chart tells you how to use the schedule to your best advantage.

THREE TO SIX MONTH
TRAINING SCHEDULE

	Level 1	Level 2	Level 3
Day			
1	25-27 min.	28-30 min.	30-33 min.
2	50-53 min.	53-55 min.	55-58 min.
3	25-27 min.	28-30 min.	30-33 min.
4	50-53 min.	53-55 min.	55-58 min.
5	25-27 min.	28-30 min.	30-33 min.
6	60-70 min.	70-80 min.	80-90 min.
7	Make-Up Day	Make-Up Day	Make-Up Day

	Level 4	Level 5	Level 6
Day			
1	33-35 min.	35-38 min.	38-40 min.
2	58-60 min.	60-63 min.	63-65 min.
3	33-35 min.	35-38 min.	38-40 min.
4	58-60 min.	60-63 min.	63-65 min.
5	33-35 min.	35-38 min.	38-40 min.
6	90-100 min.	100-110 min.	110-120 min.
7	Make-Up Day	Make-Up Day	Make-Up Day

Schedule Guidelines

1. Do not use this chart until you have established a solid base mileage as outlined in "The Importance Of A Base." That is, you are running 20 miles a week or 30 minutes daily, comfortably.

2. Choose a marathon you want to run. Then start

THREE TO SIX MONTH
TRAINING SCHEDULE (CON'T)

Day	Level 7	Level 8	Level 9
1	40-43 min.	43-45 min.	45-48 min.
2	65-70 min.	70-75 min.	75-80 min.
3	40-43 min.	43-45 min.	45-48 min.
4	65-70 min.	70-75 min.	75-80 min.
5	40-43 min.	43-45 min.	45-48 min.
6	120 min.	120 min.	120-135 min.
7	Make-Up Day	Make-Up Day	Make-Up Day

Day	Level 10	Level 11	Level 12
1	48 min.	48 min.	48 min.
2	80 min.	80 min.	80 min.
3	48 min.	48 min.	48 min.
4	80 min.	80 min.	80 min.
5	48 min.	48 min.	48 min.
6	135-150 min.	150-165 min.	150 min.
7	Make-Up Day	Make-Up Day	Make-Up Day

this schedule three to six months before the marathon. Three months if you have been running base mileage for a year or more. Six months if you have been running base mileage for less than a year.

3. Spend one week at each level if you follow the three month plan. Two weeks at each level if you are going to follow the six month plan.

8 MINUTE PACE
TRAINING SCHEDULE

	Level 1	Level 2	Level 3
Day			
1	3.1-3.5 mi.	3.5-3.7 mi.	3.7-4.1 mi.
2	6.4-6.7 mi.	6.7-6.9 mi.	6.9-7.2 mi.
3	3.1-3.5 mi.	3.5-3.7 mi.	3.7-4.1 mi.
4	6.4-6.7 mi.	6.7-6.9 mi.	6.9-7.2 mi.
5	3.1-3.5 mi.	3.5-3.7 mi.	3.7-4.1 mi.
6	7.8-8.8 mi.	8.8-10.0 mi.	10.0-11.2 mi.
7	Make-Up Day	Make-Up Day	Make-Up Day

	Level 4	Level 5	Level 6
Day			
1	4.1-4.4 mi.	4.4-4.8 mi.	4.8-5.0 mi.
2	7.2-7.5 mi.	7.5-7.9 mi.	7.9-8.1 mi.
3	4.1-4.4 mi.	4.4-4.8 mi.	4.8-5.0 mi.
4	7.2-7.5 mi.	7.5-7.9 mi.	7.9-8.1 mi.
5	4.1-4.4 mi.	4.4-4.8 mi.	4.8-5.0 mi.
6	11.2-12.8 mi.	12.8-13.8 mi.	13.8-15.0 mi.
7	Make-Up Day	Make-Up Day	Make-Up Day

4. If you are currently running more than 35 minutes a day, 6 days a week you are permitted to start at a higher level. For example, if you are running 40 minutes a day start at Level 2, 45 minutes a day start at Level 3; 50 minutes a day start at Level 5; 55 minutes a day start at Level 7; and 60 minutes a day start at Level 8.

8 MINUTE PACE
TRAINING SCHEDULE (CON'T)

	Level 7	Level 8	Level 9
Day			
1	5.0-5.3 mi.	5.3-5.6 mi.	5.6-6.0 mi.
2	8.1-8.7 mi.	8.7-9.2 mi.	9.2-10.0 mi.
3	5.0-5.3 mi.	5.3-5.6 mi.	5.6-6.0 mi.
4	8.1-8.7 mi.	8.7-9.2 mi.	9.2-10.0 mi.
5	5.0-5.3 mi.	5.3-5.6 mi.	5.6-6.0 mi.
6	15.0 mi.	15.0 mi.	15.0-17.5 mi.
7	Make-Up Day	Make-Up Day	Make-Up Day

	Level 10	Level 11	Level 12
Day			
1	6 mi.	6 mi.	6 mi.
2	10 mi.	10 mi.	10 mi.
3	6 mi.	6 mi.	6 mi.
4	10 mi.	10 mi.	10 mi.
5	6 mi.	6 mi.	6 mi.
6	15.0-17.5 mi.	17.5-20.0 mi.*	17.5 mi.
7	Make-Up Day	Make-Up Day	Make-Up Day

Please remember these times are based on the assumption that you are running a mile at an 8 minute pace. If you're going to run faster then your mileage would be greater. If you're going to run slower, your mileage would be less.
*Do not run further than 20 miles.

5. The make-up day is to be just that. It can also be a rest day. Do not use it as an extra day for more mileage unless you are coming up short for a particular week.

6. The schedule is predicated on an easy/hard cycle. That is one day you go short and the next day you go long. This pattern gives your body a chance to recover from the longer runs.

7. Run each day at the pace you expect to run the marathon. No faster or slower. If your goal is to run a marathon in 3½ hours then you'll run your miles at about an 8 minute pace.

8. The minute range on the chart can be used in two ways: a) the range can give you the latitude to run a little longer or shorter on selected days, or b) if you select the six month sequence, you can spend one week on the lower side of the range and the second week on the higher side of the range at each particular level.

9. If you prefer, mileage can be used in place of minutes. That is, select the pace you want to run the marathon. Determine how many miles you can run in the recommended length of time on the schedule. The chart entitled "8 Minute Pace Training Schedule" is based on mileage at about an 8 minute pace.

10. Enter some races to help you through your longer run days. Two or three times during a three month period of time is super. It will give you the flavor of the marathon and teach you something about pace. The race will also build your confidence. Do not, however, approach these runs seriously. They are to be done to give you company when running long distances, and to give you better feelings about your upcoming marathon. If you feel you are too competitive and fear you will run these as hard races, do not enter. These races can wipe you out and affect your ultimate performance in the marathon.

11. Under no circumstances are you to run further than 20 miles. If you follow our marathon plan you will be able to run 26 miles.

12. The last week prior to the marathon is not included on this schedule. This is considered a taper-off week. We suggest that Level 13 be a reduced mileage week. We advocate four days of 30 minute runs, and then, three days of complete rest or, if you prefer, light 15 to 20 minute runs.

We feel the CONSUMER GUIDE® magazine marathon plan is not only effective but one you can live with. That is important in this busy world. You compete with yourself and not against an arbitrary set of standards that may be, for one reason or another, inappropriate for you as an individual. You decide your own pace of running, your own rate of improvements, and your own marathon.

Importance Of Warming Up And Cooling Down

Of course, the length of time running does not include your warm-up and cool-down time. These are also important ingredients in the CONSUMER GUIDE® magazine marathon plan. Both will aid your performance and then will help make your running less painful.

Warming Up

When you go to a track meet, you watch the events. Most of the time you pay little attention to the other activities that are going on down the field. But if you look carefully you will see the polevaulters doing 10 quick push-ups, several racers jogging leisurely around the track, and the javelin thrower taking a few practice throws. You'll also notice that all the athletes, be they entered in field or track events, are doing a lot of slow stretching. These athletes are doing what everyone knows they should do; that is warm up prior to the actual competition itself. These athletes know that they have to warm up, to get their muscles loosened and limbered, and their hearts and lungs pumping.

This is true for every sport. Football players, tennis players, volleyball players, even serious table tennis players go through various forms of warm-up exercises designed to work on the specific muscles, ligaments, tendons, and joints that will absorb the stress of their particular activity.

It is just as important for the marathoner. The marathoner needs to be concerned about preparing his muscular and skeletal systems for more vigorous exercise. He may also want to do some fast walking to prepare his cardiovascular system, but quite frankly he can use the first few miles of the marathon as the warm up.

Research has shown the best kinds of exercises for the marathoner are slow stretching exercises. That is, you will want to do a series of flexibility exercises that will enable the various parts of the body to handle the rigors of running. You should consider your whole body, even your neck, shoulders, and arms. Particular attention should be paid to the muscles of the legs.

The primary purpose of the warm up should be to stretch the muscles and joints to their full extent without straining. The stretching should be done in a slow fashion, not a ballistic movement.

There are all kinds of exercises that you can do to warm up for running.

The exercises that follow are considered excellent for the marathoner. They will put the muscles and tendons under proper stretch and thereby permit improvement of flexibility—something which is lost with the repetitive pattern of running. Approximately 10 to 15 minutes seems to be an adequate amount of time to compensate for all the running you'll do.

These are the exercises to be done before doing your running. Do these exercises in the order listed. These activities will loosen muscle groups, and prepare the joints for more vigorous exercise. With these exercises, go to the "point of stretch." That is, if you go any further you will feel pain. Once you're at that point, do not bounce. Hold for 10 seconds. Over the weeks, you can increase to 30 seconds maximum. While stretching, concentrate on relaxing the muscles being stretched.

These stretching exercises can then be followed with a few minutes of walking, or slow running prior to the actual training runs.

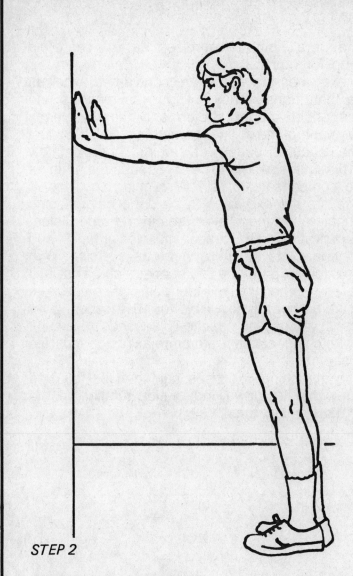

STEP 2

Calf/Tendon Stretch

1. Stand about two to three feet away from the wall.
2. Lean forward, with your body straight. Place your palms against the wall at eye level.

STEP 3

3. Step backward. Continue to support your weight with your hands. Remain flat-footed until you feel your calf muscles stretching.

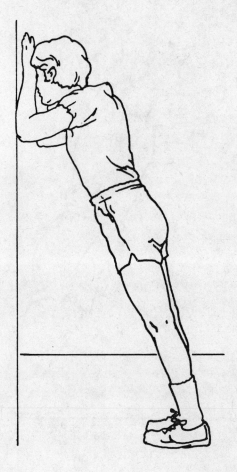

STEP 1

Calf/Achilles Stretch

1. Face a wall or corner—anything you can lean against. Stand a few feet away from the wall. Rest your forearms on it, and place your forehead on the back of your hands.

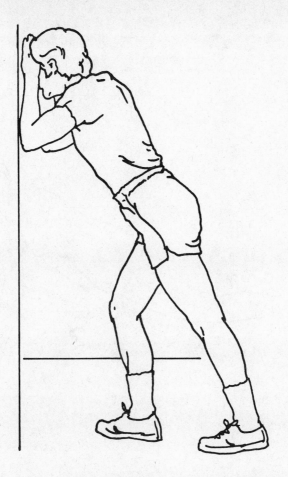

STEP 2

2. Bend your right knee, and bring it toward the wall. Keep your left leg straight. Be certain that your left heel remains on the floor. Keep your toes pointed straight ahead. Hold. You should feel the stretching in your calf.

3. Bend the left knee. Hold. You should feel the stretching in your Achilles tendon.

4. Repeat with your other leg.

STEP 2

Sprinter

1. Assume a squatting position on the floor.
2. Extend one leg backward as far as possible. Your hands should be touching the floor. Hold.
3. Repeat with the other leg.

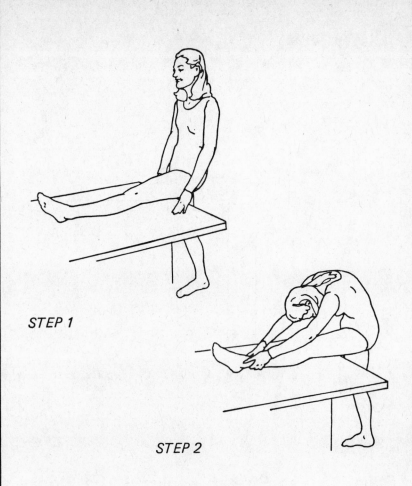

STEP 1

STEP 2

Standing Leg Stretch

1. Find a chair or table approximately three feet in height. Place one foot on the table so that the knee is straight and the leg is parallel to the floor.

2. Slowly extend your fingertips toward the out-stretched leg on the table. Eventually you should be able to get your forehead to your knee.

3. Repeat with the other leg.

STEP 2

Standing Leg Stretch—Toward The Floor

1. Stand sideward to the same chair or table mentioned in the preceding exercise. Place one foot on the table so that the knee is straight and the leg is parallel to the floor. The inside of the outstretched leg should be resting on the table.

2. Slowly bend at your waist and extend your fingertips toward the foot on the floor. Hold.

3. Return to upright position.

4. Repeat with the other leg.

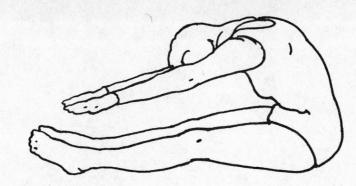

STEP 1

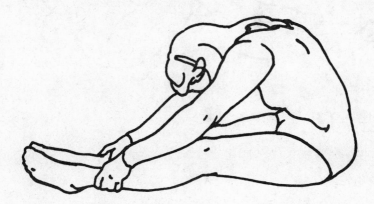

STEP 2

Sitting Toe Touches

1. Sit on the floor with your legs extended in front of you, feet together.

2. Reach for your toes with both hands, and bring your forehead as close to your knees as possible.

3. Return to sitting position.

STEP 4

Spinal Stretch

1. Sit on the floor with your legs straight in front of you.

2. With your right leg straight, put your left foot on the floor on the other side of your right knee.

3. Reach over your left leg with your right arm so that your elbow is on the outside of your left leg.

4. Twist your upper body to the left, pushing with your right elbow on the outside of your left knee. Hold.

5. Repeat on the other side.

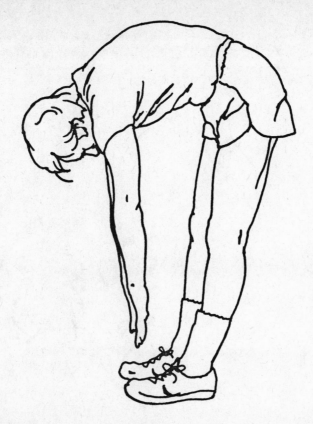

STEP 2

Back Stretch

1. Stand erect with your feet shoulder-width apart.
2. Bend forward slowly at the waist. Let your arms, shoulders, and neck relax. Stretch until you feel a slight pull in the muscles on the back of your legs.
3. If you cannot touch the floor, place your hands on the backs of your legs. That will give you support. Hold. Remember, when you come back up, bend your knee to take the pressure off your lower back.
4. Return to an upright position.

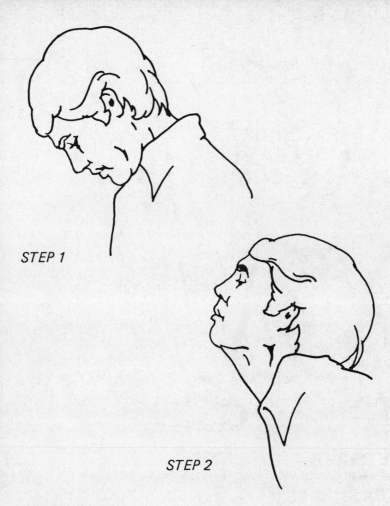

STEP 1

STEP 2

Head Flexor

1. Assume a standing position with your arms at your sides. Flex your head forward by dropping the chin to your chest. Try to draw your chin down as far as possible.

2. Extend your head backward as far as possible. This exercise improves neck flexibility and also can help firm muscles in the front of the neck.

3. Return to starting position.

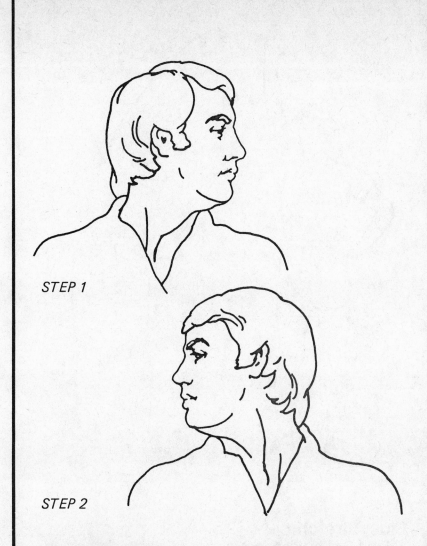

STEP 1

STEP 2

Neck Turns

1. Assume a standing position with your arms at sides. Turn your head to the left, and look over your left shoulder.
2. Turn it to the right and look over your right shoulder. This exercise is good for neck flexibility.

STEP 2   *STEP 3*

Side Stretch

1. Stand with your feet about shoulder-width apart. Keep your legs straight.
2. Place one hand on your hip, and extend your other arm up and over your head.
3. Bend to the side on which your hand is placed on hip. Move slowly. Hold.
4. Repeat on the other side.

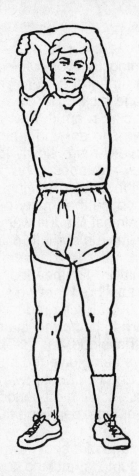

STEP 2

Shoulder Stretch

1. Assume a standing position with feet about shoulder-width apart.

2. With both arms over your head, hold the elbow of one arm with the hand of the other arm. Slowly pull the elbow behind your head. Do not force. Hold.

3. Repeat on the other side.

Cooling Down

At the same track meet where all those runners and jumpers are warming up, you will see the distance racers cooling down after their run. They don't simply stop, walk over, and pick up a medal if they win or amble off to the locker room if they lose. They know from experience what to do, and they continue to run after the race is over—more slowly to be sure. They even walk. But they are tapering off from the running experience. After the slower running or walking, you will probably also notice that many of them do some mild calisthenics. Almost like the warm up in reverse.

Stopping a vigorous run abruptly can be dangerous. Sudden relaxation after a demanding session of running can result in lightheadedness, dizziness, nausea, and even fainting. What we advise strongly is that you come out of your run gradually and smoothly. Let your body return to its normal state at a moderate rate. Remember the blood has been going to your muscles and now is being diverted back to its normal circulation pattern and you do not want the shift to be too abrupt. Without a cooling-off period, blood will pool in the feet and lower legs, depriving the brain of much needed oxygen.

The other advantage of a cool down is that it allows you to again do some stretching to counteract the effect of the repetitive running action. Again, you can use the same exercises we recommended in warming up for the cool down.

In summation what we've been saying here is simple. The running experience should be a three-part cycle: warm up; run; cool down. The first and last of these three do not need to be long, drawn-out affairs. They should be short and effective, and natural.

The Marathon As An Energy Crisis

by Carl Foster

The marathon is unique. Regardless of how much you have trained or raced previously, the sheer length of a marathon presents challenges unlike any within the spectrum of long-distance running. The more relaxed pace of the marathon may at first give you the impression of a relatively easy event. But there is no way to conceive how long the last five miles can be until you have completed a run of this length. In running a marathon, your body must adapt to physiological challenges that are likely to be new to you. The biggest of these may be thought of as analogous to an automobile running out of fuel at the end of a journey. An understanding of this before the event begins can contribute to your success. It can also make the difference between a relatively pleasant, if strenuous, physical challenge and the thoroughly miserable experience a bad marathon can become. An understanding of some basic physiology will help you appreciate the basic problem encountered in marathon running. It will also set the stage for understanding how some of the short term dietary manipulations used by marathon runners work.

Fuel For The Run

The most basic requirement for all human movement is the contraction of the skeletal muscles. Without that, no purposeful movement can take place. The organization and forcefulness of muscular contraction dictates whether I blink my eye, write an article for marathon runners, or run. For skeletal muscles to contract for more than a few seconds at a time, a continuing source of energy is needed. In humans, and virtually all other animals, the primary source of new energy is the oxidation (or burning) of fuel in the presence of oxygen. A common example of this is the burning of a log (fuel) in your fireplace using the oxygen in the room, air. Energy (light and heat) are released and channeled for your use (warming your house). Within our bodies the "fireplaces" are the mitochondria within each cell. The fuel is either carbohydrate or fat, and oxygen, which is transported to the mitochondria from the room air through the combined actions of your lungs, heart, and blood. Energy (in the chemical form—ATP) is released for contracting your skeletal muscles.

Using the fireplace analogy again, you should note that by using a bellows to provide more oxygen, you can make the fire burn hotter (release energy at a higher rate). But you must still continually add fuel for the fire to continue burning. In a similar fashion, if you want to run at a faster pace, more energy is required. That means you need more oxygen and you are forced to breathe harder and have your heart beat faster. For exercise to continue, fuel must also be made available continually. This fuel may take the form of carbohydrates, available either as glycogen (a stored form of carbohydrates) in the skeletal muscles, or as glucose circulating in the blood. Fat, which in humans is stored mostly just beneath the skin (and often in embarrassing quantities about the waist) can also serve as a fuel for muscular contraction. It is usually available as free fatty acids circulating in the blood. The use of fat as fuel demands the continual release of fatty acids from their storage sites and their delivery to the muscle tissue.

During heavy exercise, such as marathon running, carbohydrates are the preferred fuel. There are two reasons for this: 1) carbohydrates, in the form of muscle glycogen, are already available in the muscle cell. So, the delivery of the fuel to the "fireplace" is rather a simple process. Fats, on the other hand, must be released from storage in the fat tissue (a generally slow process), transported to the muscles, and taken into the cell before they can be used as fuel. 2) Carbohydrates are a more efficient fuel than fats. Carbohydrates burning yield more energy per unit of oxygen consumed than that derived from fats. Since the availability of oxygen during exercise is often limited, the slightly greater efficiency of carbohydrates as a fuel is important.

For reasons that are still not fully understood, the depletion of the muscle carbohydrate stores (which typically occurs after about two hours of running at marathon pace) is associated with a marked feeling of fatigue. That feeling is often referred to as "the wall." The fatigue is rather different from the fatigue experienced in shorter races and has been variously described as "weariness," "losing the urge to run" or "heaviness." Some of you may have experienced this feeling after several consecutive days of heavy training. If you've never experienced this type of fatigue previously you may be in for a shock. The first sensations of muscle glycogen depletion can be most disconcerting. The experience of muscle glycogen depletion is usually associated with a slowing of the pace of running. Because of the great length of the marathon, even small changes in pace will have a remarkable effect on total time. Accordingly, the final result in a marathon race is determined almost as much by the slowdown at the end of the marathon as by the initial pace during the early miles. For example, a novice marathon runner may run the first 15 miles at 7:15/mile (representing 3:10 for a full marathon). But he slows to 8:00/mile for the next 5 miles (a 3:32

pace). In the final 6.2 miles he logs a 9:00/mile (a 3:56 pace). This marathoner would find his overall time of 3:24 a long way from the original pace he thought was reasonable and comfortable.

What then of the wall? Is running out of fuel inevitable? Is there a way to prevent the slowdown? In 1939, the Scandinavian physiologists Christensen and Hansen noted that the composition of a subject's recent diet had a marked influence on how long the subject was able to continue heavy exercise. Diets rich in carbohydrates improved the subject's ability to continue exercise at a fixed pace. Diets poor in carbohydrates, on the other hand, were associated with a reduced ability to exercise. Some years later, another group of Scandinavian physiologists determined that the relative composition of an athlete's diet was closely related to the concentration of glycogen in the skeletal muscles. They further noted that exhaustion occurred when the muscle glycogen concentration was very low. Obviously then, a carbohydrate-rich diet increases the total score of muscle glycogen. The increased amount of muscle glycogen delays the time when critically low concentrations of muscle glycogen are reached. So, the length of time it takes for a person to reach or hit the wall is increased. To use an automotive analogy, diets rich in carbohydrates act to increase the capacity of our fuel tanks thus increasing our cruising range.

Carbohydrate Loading

With this understanding of increased muscle glycogen and better physical performance, scientists, coaches, and athletes have inaugurated the age of carbohydrate loading. The practice of carbohydrate loading and more recent developments in our under-standing of sports nutrition have made modest but significant improvements in marathon performance. More importantly, however, these developments have added greatly to the ease of running the first marathon. How then does carbohydrate loading work? If I am to race on Saturday, what do I eat to help myself do better?

In general carbohydrate loading works on the premise that the muscle glycogen stores are depleted by a long run. That is followed by reloading these stores with a combination of light exercise and a diet relatively rich in carbohydrates. This regimen appears to produce a "bounce" in the muscle glycogen concentration. That is to say, by first depleting the glycogen stores you can temporarily attain unusually high values for muscle glycogen for a short time after refilling the stores. The height of this bounce appears to be related to the magnitude of depletion (the length of your last long run) and the length of time before reloading occurs. In other words, depleting the gly-cogen stores and staying depleted for a couple of days works somewhat better than simply depleting alone. A simplified plan for carbohydrate loading is presented in the following chart.

SIMPLIFIED PLAN FOR CARBOHYDRATE LOADING

Sunday	15-20 mile long run
Monday	Medium run, avoid carbohy-drates
Tuesday	Medium run, avoid carbohy-drates

SIMPLIFIED PLAN FOR
CARBOHYDRATE LOADING (con't)

Wednesday	Easy run, eat plenty of carbohydrates
Thursday	Easy run, eat plenty of carbohydrates
Friday	Very easy run, eat plenty of carbohydrates
Saturday	Race

Since the process of staying depleted is usually somewhat difficult, a modified carbohydrate loading procedure is often recommended for the first time marathoner. This modified procedure would be as follows:

MODIFIED PLAN FOR
CARBOHYDRATE LOADING

Tuesday	15-20 mile long run
Wednesday	Easy run, eat plenty of carbohydrates
Thursday	Easy run, eat plenty of carbohydrates
Friday	Very easy run, eat plenty of carbohydrates
Saturday	Race

It is important to remember that the dietary goal is to change the *relative proportions* of one's diet during the days preceding a race. Far too often, carbohydrate loading is thought of as an excuse to go on a dietary binge. That is trouble. If you overeat you'll feel like the day after Thanksgiving when you come to the starting line. Don't gorge yourself with cookies, donuts, pizza, and beer. A relatively normal diet with somewhat reduced quantities of meat and dairy products and proportionally increased quantities of vegetables, fruit, and bread is best. If sweets are to be eaten they should be in the form of hard candy. Foods like ice cream, chocolate, and cakes contain large amounts of fat, a constituent not necessary in the marathoner's diet during the days preceding a race. If you choose to use the longer carbohydrate loading pattern, then the amount of vegetables, fruit, and bread in your diet should be markedly reduced during the carbohydrate free portion of the diet.

During the carbohydrate loading period it is very important to reduce the training load. It does very little good to eat large amounts of carbohydrates if you use them up during the next day's training. You must realize that you will gain far more from the muscle glycogen loading resulting from 3 to 4 days of relative rest than from the minimal additional conditioning you might gain with 3 or 4 days extra training. I prefer to run only 1-2 miles a day during this period. I feel better following an easy run than following a day of complete rest. However, many successful marathoners rest completely during the days preceding a race with generally good results. You must decide which is best for you.

Carbohydrate loading is an extremely useful tool for the marathon runner. It should, however, be viewed as a *subtle variation from your normal diet-activity pattern.* Your diet should still be balanced but with a shift toward more carbohydrates and less fat and protein. This shift in dietary pattern should be associated with a reduction in your training load. Training during this period should be at most only a few miles a day. A complete stoppage of training for 1-3 days should be considered as a distinct possibility. Remember, that the positive effect of carbohydrate loading is to minimize the slowdown at the end of the race. It is not to allow a faster pace early in the race. Carbohydrate loading represents a deviation from your normal dietary pattern. For some people a gastrointestinal upset may occur. Since one of your primary goals is to arrive at the starting line rested, relaxed and feeling fit, you should be aware of the possibility of this upset. Accordingly, a practice loading session should be tried during the weeks before the actual race.

Carbohydrate Sparing And Wasting

The traditional approach to the fuel problem in marathon running has been to attempt to enlarge the total store of glycogen. In other words, creating a larger fuel tank. In the fuel-conscious '70s, it is appropriate that a substantial amount of research has been directed toward understanding factors which influence the *rate* at which muscle glycogen is used. In short, how to improve gas mileage.

The studies have generally indicated that the rate at which glycogen is used is probably as important as the total size of the glycogen stores. Recent experiments have shown that the runner's diet just before the run can have a profound influence upon the rate of glycogen use.

In an effort to improve the carbohydrate loading process some runners believe that extra carbohydrates should be eaten right up to the start of the race. Research shows that this is not a good idea. Release of insulin into the blood following the eating of carbohydrates acts to block the release of fatty acids from the fat tissue. That means there is a decrease in the concentration of circulating fatty acids. Consequently, muscle glycogen and blood glucose are the *only* fuels potentially available for muscular contraction. During the run, an increased rate of muscle glycogen use occurs and there is a rapid initial drop in blood glucose. If the running is continued, fatigue from muscle glycogen depletion occurs at a rate faster than normal. Also, in a few people blood glucose continues to fall until hypoglycemia occurs. Hypoglycemia produces overpowering weariness, lightheadedness, irritability, and occasionally, fainting. Those feelings occur when the blood glucose level falls to a point where the fuel supply to the brain becomes limited.

The unfavorable response to immediate pre-running feedings appears to be alleviated by the insulin secreted in response to the carbohydrates in a meal. If a meal is eaten far enough in advance to allow complete digestion, the insulin levels will be normal. So the fatty acids are not blocked. In most cases a meal 3-6 hours before the marathon run will allow adequate depletion. Since most marathons are started in the morning, the most practical solution to the pre-run feeding problem is to eat your last meal during the evening. That way you'll come to the starting line with an empty stomach. For midday races, breakfast should be very *light* and eaten as many hours before the race as possible. The practice of early eating will improve your "fuel economy."

Liquids And Electrolytes

In addition to providing a continuing source of fuel during a marathon, the runner must also find a means of regulating his body temperature. For the most part, the regulation of body temperature depends upon sweating. And the sweating depends on the maintenance and adequate volume of blood plasma. Drinking water during running has been shown to help maintain body temperature. Within reason, the larger the volume of water consumed during a race, the lower the body temperature. Since sweat also contains quantities of electrolytes, some commercially available drinks designed for the runner contain small quantities of electrolytes (sodium and potassium).

Since the blood glucose concentration tends to fall during several hours of exercise, many commercially available drinks contain quantities of glucose with the intention of supporting the blood glucose level. Let's take a look at the effect of adding electrolytes and glucose to a drink.

Sweat is hypotonic. That means, relatively more water than salt is lost during the course of a race. The body is very good at conserving electrolytes. So a serious salt shortage is unlikely to develop during the course of a marathon race. The simplest solution to the water replacement problem during marathon running appears to be *water*. Again, you might wish to experiment with various combinations of water or commercially available athletic drinks during practice. That way you'll find a solution that leaves you feeling best during long training runs.

During a long run, blood glucose falls steadily. After three to four hours, values low enough to cause symptoms of hypoglycemia (weariness, lightheadedness, irritability) begin to develop. A traditional approach to solving this problem has been the drinking of glucose-containing drinks during the course of the run. To some extent this strategy is useful. But, the presence of glucose in a beverage slows the rate at which the beverage leaves the stomach. In fact, beverages with enough glucose to significantly influence the blood glucose leave the stomach so slowly that their contribution to either blood glucose or to water balance is relatively small. Since the importance of water ingestion during marathon running is much greater than that of glucose, any factor interfering with the delivery of water to the system must be used with great caution. If you think you will be on the course for more than four hours, the importance of glucose in your drink increases. Hypoglycemia may become a problem even more important than dehydration. Changing drinks to a weak glucose solution may be justified after about three hours of running. But commercially available athletic drinks may be too concentrated and interfere with water and glucose delivery. Since a considerable volume of fluid is also likely to be trapped in the stomach, these solutions may cause an upset stomach. It is probably wisest to dilute with an equal amount of water whatever drink is being offered by the race sponsors. That practice should allow the delivery of small amounts of glucose to your blood while insuring maximal delivery of water to the system.

The physiological responses to the drinking of fluid during marathon running are pretty much proportional to the volume of fluid drunk. That holds true whether water or a glucose-electrolyte solution is used. The simplest way to get relatively large volumes of fluid is to take frequent small drinks rather than a few large drinks. Larger volumes of fluid increase the chance of gastric distress.

The drinking of fluids during marathon running is very important. The increase in body temperature, dehydration, and hypoglycemia may all be controlled partially, through a wise use of liquids during exercise. In general, the more fluid you can drink without causing an upset stomach the better. The need for electrolytes during a single bout of exercise is probably quite small. Furthermore, since glucose-containing beverages may slow the emptying of the stomach and contribute to gastric distress, the best possible solution appears to be ordinary water. In the case of slower runners who may expect to be on the course for more than about four hours, a very weak glucose solution may be helpful. In practical terms this probably means diluting most commercially available drinks by about half. Finally, as with all other aspects of dietary manipulation, *practice in training before the event is strongly recommended.*

Other experiments have shown that some foods (tea and coffee) may influence the use of muscle glycogen.

Caffeine in coffee, and its chemical cousin theopholine in tea, have been shown to promote an increased release of fatty acids from the fat tissue. That means, muscle glycogen will be spared and slow the onset of fatigue. Some runners can expect improved performance during prolonged exercise with the aid of coffee and tea.

The technique in this case is relatively simple. About an hour before the start of competition, and at least four hours after the last meal, a strong cup of unsweetened coffee or tea is drunk. Additional doses

The drinking of fluids during marathon running is very important.

of coffee or tea may be taken during the event to magnify the effect. Theoretically, caffeine pills could be taken in place of coffee or tea. It is important to maintain a fasting state since carbohydrate feeding, right before the run, tends to block the release of fatty acids. The extra carbohydrates could make the extra coffee and tea ineffective.

Some people have objected to the use of caffeine or theopholine. They feel that these substances aren't very good for you, and, that the side effects may hurt you more than the fatty acid release may help. They argue that overdosing can happen rather easily. Furthermore, the concept of using drugs to enhance performance is contrary to the spirit of marathon running.

Although there is probably some validity to each of these arguments, the use of coffee or tea as a drink for the marathoner is not too different from using carbohydrate loading or using glucose-electrolyte drinks during the run. Their intelligent use should produce a minimum of side effects and prevent the problems of overdosing.

The potential for side effects, in using coffee or tea, suggests that you experiment with their use several times before the race. That way you'll understand the practical effects on your own body. Interestingly, in the days before the development of electrolyte-containing drinks for the athlete, marathon runners frequently drank tea as a beverage during the run. This practice was based on nothing more complicated than the observation of many runners that tea agreed with them during the race.

In summary, your eating habits can influence the rate at which your glycogen is used during running. Proper eating of certain foods can influence your endurance during marathon running.

Do not eat a lot of carbohydrates right before the marathon race. It blocks the release of fatty acids.

Eat a carbohydrate meal three to six hours before the actual race. That will give your body time to handle the insulin.

Drink coffee or tea (containing caffeine or theopholine) one hour before the race. This practice will increase the release of fatty acids, providing you with an alternative energy source.

"Practice" using coffee or tea for potential side effects, prior to the run. By the way, it's also a good idea to practice your diet manipulation prior to the run.

Summary

Most research shows that a runner's diet helps improve performance. The diet also affects the safety of the race and the pleasure-pain experienced during a marathon. The diet cannot compensate for lack of talent. It cannot make up for lack of proper training. It cannot protect you if you are foolish enough to start a race in 90 degree temperatures. But the diet can allow for small improvements in your personal performance. That is accomplished by delaying the slow down at the end of the race. So your diet can contribute to a feeling of relative ease during the race, thereby making the race a more pleasant experience. Diet can help to control the dehydration associated with marathon running. It can also contribute to regulating the rise in body temperature which is the only real health hazard presented by the marathon.

As a marathon runner you can do three things to your diet to improve performance. These are: 1) carbohydrate loading; 2) carbohydrate sparing and wasting; and 3) feeding during the run. Carbohydrate loading is the attempt to increase your total fuel reserve by a combination of reduced training and shifting the composition of the diet toward more carbohydrates during the two or three days prior to the race. This method has been shown to be pretty effective. It depends upon three basic rules: 1) a depletion run about four days before the event; 2) a reduced training load after this run to the lowest possible level; and 3) a shift in the composition of your diet to include more fruits, vegetables, and bread, and reduced quantities of meat and fat. The total calorie content of your diet should be kept at about the same level.

Carbohydrate sparing and wasting refers to attempts to change the rate at which your body uses muscle glycogen during the run. This area is still at the frontier of scientific research and very much less is known about its more practical aspects. One finding that seems to be consistant is that carbohydrate feeding within about four hours of the race may adversely affect the marathon runner. A recent carbohydrate containing meal may block the release of fatty acids from the fat tissue stores. That means the muscle glycogen stores are the only fuel available for muscular work. So there is an earlier depletion of muscle glycogen and earlier fatigue. Caffeine in coffee or the theopholine in tea can act to increase the release of fatty acids and provide another fuel for muscular work. However, the uncertain side effects from this practice indicate that these procedures should be treated cautiously. In general, you might experiment with drinking a cup of unsweetened coffee or tea about an hour before exercise. If no side effects are noted, then you might try the regimen under race conditions. The potential side effects, however, may far outweigh the benefits and the procedure should be handled cautiously.

The third strategy involves drinking during the race. Generally, the more water you can drink without upsetting your stomach the better. The value of electrolytes or glucose during the event is probably small and hardly worth the risk of an upset stomach. If you feel more comfortable with the thought of having some glucose or electrolytes during the race, use one of the commercially available athletic drinks, though it is best to dilute it first.

The key to diet manipulation by the marathon runner is common sense. The dietary strategies discussed represent only a small portion of your total race preparation. They work best if they remain subtle variations from your normal diet. And they are least likely to backfire if you try them during practice before the race.

Carl Foster is an exercise physiologist at Mt. Sinai Hospital in Milwaukee.

Coping With
The Weather

by Alan D. Claremont

Proper training will permit you to develop enough endurance and mental toughness to expect to complete your first marathon. No matter how good your training, however, bad weather conditions can have a negative effect upon your quality of training. But, if you learn to cope with the elements through proper adjustments in clothing, pace, fluid intake and behavior, you will perform better. You will have less physiological strain.

Basic Concepts Of Temperature Regulation In The Heat

When training one or two hours of long distance running you are primarily concerned with confronting and adjusting to the outdoors. Rapid changes in temperature and weather can occur abruptly, especially in the spring and fall. To train in this type of weather and remain somewhat comfortable requires a modification of clothing and behavior. These modifications must provide adequate protection against such things as temperature, wind, windchill, relative humidity, solar radiation, rain, snow, and sleet.

Successful adaptation to wide-ranging weather conditions is best achieved through an understanding of how the body handles increased body heat caused by running. The human body is only about 23 percent efficient in converting the energy of food (that you have eaten) into mechanical work (running). The remaining 77 percent of the energy is released as heat. A portion of this extra heat is used to maintain a constant body temperature—about 98.6 degrees at rest. During exercise, body temperature goes up to about 100 to 101 degrees. The increase provides the most suitable thermal environment for stimulating the rates at which your body's biochemical reactions proceed. Keeping the temperature in this range allows your body to work at optimal efficiency.

The task of controlling body temperature within proper and safe limits is very important. For example, a 150-pound athlete running a 5:30 mile pace uses about 20 calories a minute. Of the 20 calories, 15 calories or 77 percent must be eliminated as excess heat production. If you did not have this thermoregulatory system, your temperature would rise from approximately 98.6 degrees at rest to about 140 degrees during exercise. An increase of that magnitude would kill you. While your body can withstand external temperature variations of -80 to 200 degrees when adequately protected, your body can only withstand about a + or -7 degree variation in core (rectal) temperature.

Since humans are warm-blooded animals, the hot rather than the cold end of the scale is of more importance. It is easier to protect yourself from overcooling than from overheating. Even during cold weather running, the prevention of an excessive rise in core temperature is very important.

Training In The Heat And Humidity

Some of the body changes which occur during heat stress are—

1. restriction of blood flow through certain abdominal organs, and a redirection of greater circulating volume through expanded blood vessels under the skin;

2. cooling of the warm blood near the surface of the

skin as heat is withdrawn to vaporize sweat on the skin surface;

3. cooling of the skin surface through evaporative heat loss from increased sweating rates; and

4. the return of the cooled blood from the skin to the central circulation.

A proper equilibrium of heat is achieved by balancing metabolic heat production against the external avenues of heat loss—radiation, conduction, convection, and evaporation.

While this balance is remarkable, there are limits in this temperature control. Failure to regulate the increase in body temperature during running, under conditions of high temperature and/or humidity, causes the body temperature to increase in proportion to the intensity and duration of the exercise. In this situation, core temperatures may increase to the point where you may experience physical symptoms ranging from heat cramps through heat exhaustion to heat stroke.

Evaporation of sweat is the most important way to lose heat during moderate to heavy exercise. Fluid losses often exceed 1 liter (approximately 2.2 pounds) an hour. Likewise, in heavy exercise you'll lose more than 3 grams of electrolytes an hour. With such high sweat rates, body mass gradually decreases and 5 to 7 percent reductions in body weight are quite common at the finish of a marathon. Unless a runner drinks frequently and reduces his pace, progressive dehydration will occur. And the result will be impaired running performance. All this will drive the temperature up even further. That occurs because the same metabolic heat production is now being generated in a smaller body mass (weight), resulting in an increased body heat content and core temperature. Heat dissipation is also affected because of reduced sweating, and less cooling (by evaporation) at the skin surface. Core temperature elevations from 0.5 to 0.9 degrees may be expected for every 1 percent loss in body weight due to dehydration.

The rate and extent of temperature elevation during hot weather running is largely influenced by:

1. the level of metabolism: the faster you run the greater the heat production;

2. the ability of the body to dissipate extra heat mainly through the sweating mechanism; and

3. the extent to which the body dehydrates.

If you understand these basic facts you'll know the proper preventive steps to successfully contend with heat stress conditions during training and racing. Remember these guidelines:

1. Heat Stress Illness: An added strain is placed upon the cardiovascular system since the muscles and skin must share a limited circulating blood volume. The result is a greater sensation of fatigue during hot weather running. You should recognize the warning signs of heat sickness. They are faintness, nausea, headache, disorientation, pale cold skin, or a decrease in sweat rate. If these symptoms persist you should *reduce your pace* as necessary *or stop*. Locate a shady spot, if possible. Rest with your legs elevated for as long as necessary. Usually 20 to 30 minutes will do. Drink cool liquids when available. A few years ago I participated in a five mile race in 97 degrees—80 percent relative humidity. I erroneously thought the distance was too short to cause heat problems. Two runners required immediate emergency medical care. They collapsed within minutes of finishing. Most participants required surveillance for some time after the race. Fortunately, a nearby shallow stream provided me with relief and a rapid recovery. My excess heat was rapidly conducted away by the cool flowing water. The day's experience provided a lasting impression and recognition of just how rapidly heat disorders can develop in a competitive situation under less than desirable weather conditions. The symptoms of heat exhaustion occurred in less than 30 minutes.

The symptoms of heat stress illness are of even greater concern to the less well-trained athlete. The less training you have, the greater the susceptibility and the lower the tolerance to such conditions. A less fit person must be prepared to slow down to a running speed that will confine metabolic heat production to levels within the current capacity of the thermoregulatory system to maintain thermal balance. A particularly bad time of year in the Midwest for heat disorders is during competitions held on an unexpectedly hot day in April or early May. Most runners have been training in typically cool seasonal temperatures. Their bodies are not acclimated to the sudden hot change. There is also a tendency to underestimate the changing weather conditions and give less thought to appropriate adjustments beforehand. Be ultracautious on these occasions. Please recognize that it requires 12 to 14 days of daily exposures to heat stress conditions before becoming acclimated.

2. Fluid Intake:

(a) Day To Day: It is quite possible to lose a liter of sweat (2.2 pounds) an hour during training in 90 degree weather. Weight reductions of 6 to 9 pounds over the marathon distance are not uncommon. On a day-to-day basis, restoration of fluid and electrolyte losses (mainly sodium and chloride) is necessary. The fluid and electrolytes will help maintain normal body functions and permit regular training. Fluid deficits can usually be made up between training sessions by drinking appropriate amounts of preferred beverages. Liberal salting of a balanced dietary intake of foodstuffs is generally sufficient for replacement of electrolytes. Yet, as frequently occurs with industrial employees working in hot environments (e.g., foundry, steel mill), it is possible for a runner to reach a chronic state of dehydration. Over a period of days, dehydration may also be accompanied by a depletion of electrolytes. That is because the thirst mechanism is usually satiated before adequate fluid volumes have been restored. It is, therefore, usually necessary to force drink even though you're not thirsty. That way, proper fluid balance will be maintained. A simple check on the state of hydration is to weigh yourself after each and immediately prior to the next workout. Your weight should be comparable.

(b) On The Run: The recent position statement on fluid intakes during distance running by the American College of Sports Medicine recommends that fluid stations be located at 2.25 to 3.0 mile intervals. The drinking of 13 to 17 ounces of fluid before starting out and at the specified intervals is suggested. Cold water, rather than sugar solutions, is the preferred beverage. Glucose concentrations in excess of 2.5

percent severely impair the rate of emptying from the stomach. The glucose may even contribute to hydration by drawing fluid into the stomach to dilute the sugar solution before absorption into the bloodstream can occur.

The main electrolytes lost in sweat are sodium, potassium, and chlorine. These ions are not depleted enough during any one particular training session or race to warrant supplemental replacement. Thus, commercial glucose solutions fortified with electrolytes would appear unnecessary. Liberal salting with attention to foods rich in potassium will help guard against potentially excessive electrolyte losses during longer periods of hot weather training.

3. Promoting Heat Loss: With improved physical conditioning and adequate fluid intake, the body's sweating response is increased. What else can be done to increase the effectiveness of this most important avenue of heat loss in exercise? Simply wear, within the constraints of decency, *as little* clothing as possible. Expose a *maximum* of skin surface area for evaporation of sweat. Clothing which inhibits evaporation inhibits heat loss. Sweat that drips off is non-effective. If confronted with an early morning race or training run in which the prevailing temperatures initially indicate "T-shirt comfort" during warm-up, be assured that your increased heat production and the increase in environmental temperature will make you overdressed. Personal experience has evolved the practice of discarding the top and feeling chilly for the first 8 to 10 minutes. I'm soon comfortably warm but not "too warm" as might occur if sweat evaporation were impeded by unnecessary clothing over the large surface area of the trunk.

For warm weather runs, expose a maximum of skin for sweat evaporation.

The worst conditions for heat loss are high temperatures and relative humidities. Substantial sweat drippage occurs despite minimal attire because the water vapor in the atmosphere is already very high, thus lowering its capacity to hold more moisture. Under these conditions, I always take advantage of upper body spraying from foresighted hose-bearing bystanders. I also always pour water over my head at aid stations.

Running A Marathon In The Heat

Nevertheless, the ability to survive high internal temperatures is a prerequisite to successful distance running. Rectal (core) temperatures ranging from 102 to 106 degrees indicate that the standard of performance is influenced by the metabolic heat load associated with increased muscular metabolism. In 1966, the winner of the Whitney English Marathon had a rectal temperature of 106 degrees. In addition, seven other runners had rectal temperatures greater than 104 degrees. The greatest proportion of competitors, however, placing well back in the field, produced temperatures ranging between 103 and 104 degrees. Responses from nationally ranked marathoners have indicated that severe subjective stress is experienced when temperatures rise above 104 degrees. Amby Burfoot, however, won the 1968 Boston Marathon while enduring a heat load increase to 105.3 degrees without apparent ill effects.

It is very important to remember that each runner is a unique individual physiologically. So runners may vary considerably in their responses to a heat stress situation. In particular, the older the person, the less fit, and the unacclimated runner will generally show a

To promote heat loss in high humidity, pour water over your head at aid stations.

more pronounced behavioral and physiologic response to high environmental temperatures and/or humidity. They will sweat less, drink less, and exhibit higher body temperatures. I urge the less experienced runner to be particularly conservative in his approach toward running a marathon in the heat. Do not get caught up in the mass enthusiasm of the event and permit your initial pace to be too fast. The inevitable will occur. The event may degenerate into a potentially health hazardous ordeal rather than a satisfying and rewarding experience. Plan your race well. And give due consideration to previous hot weather experiences, anticipated weather conditions, running attire, and fluid requirements.

Training In The Cold

The lower end of the seasonal temperature scale can be a hassle. Winds and slippery underfooting may discourage even the most hardy and dedicated runners, at times. What is important to realize, however, is that with appropriate adjustments for climatic conditions during the winter season, an athlete does not have to forsake a training session. Training can be continued with minimal cold discomfort because of man's ability to avoid overcooling. You can surround yourself in a biologically preferred semitropic microclimate with adequate protective clothing. In addition, reduced blood flow to the skin from constriction of surface blood vessels and lower skin temperatures greatly increase the insulative capacity of the outer body "shell." These adjustments further minimize convection and radiative thermal transfer which are major avenues for heat loss at lower ambient temperatures. Nevertheless, physiological cold adjustments are not well understood and of little practical advantage compared to field experience and knowing how to dress appropriately to avoid the potential dangers associated with sudden cooling. Even a small drop in internal body temperatures can cause marked shivering with severe impairment to coordinated muscular movements.

Protected within a microclimate of warm clothing, it is possible to participate enjoyably in many activities such as cross-country skiing, hill climbing, backpacking, running, etc., that may involve extended exposure to the cold. Unfortunately, there are certain environmental conditions that may exceed the capacity of the thermoregulatory systems. The hazards of cold, windy, wet weather deserve special attention. Varying combinations of these adversities have been associated with over 40 documented fatalities during hill climbing expeditions in New Zealand and England (1890-1960). The participants of these annual expeditions were often exposed to cold, windy, wet weather while hiking for several hours in the hills. Although providing sufficient warmth when dry, the insulative value of the clothing was reduced when it became wet. The most probable cause of these recorded cold deaths was later determined in a series of environmental chamber experiments. The noted English environmental physiologist, L.G. Pugh, observed volunteer subjects who walked under simulated conditions of wet clothing, cold and wind. Pugh noted that hill walkers habitually travel at 50 to 60 percent of their maximum walking capacity. Well-conditioned individuals can sustain a fast enough pace to produce enough metabolic heat and keep warm despite the lower insulative value of wet clothing. On the other hand, slow and/or fatigued walkers do not produce sufficient heat to maintain thermal equilibrium. The result is gradual body cooling to the point of loss of coordinated muscular movement. Increasing fatigue with further deterioration of pace accelerates the rate of body cooling followed by the onset of collapse within 1 to 2 hours. In the field, walkers totally exhausted, either collapsed or sat down awaiting rescue personnel who were unable to arrive in sufficient time to save them from cold (hypothermic) death.

Fortunately, these weather extremes are not frequent and when they do occur, need not interfere with regular running. Proper clothing will maintain warm comfort. Special precautions should be taken to avoid becoming lost in relatively uninhabited surroundings. As you tire, running rates may deteriorate so that your heat loss to the environment is greater than your heat production. That situation can lead to hypothermia after one to two hours exposure. Running along frequently travelled routes and informing others of your intended running course minimizes the possibility of becoming stranded.

Some people fear that "cold air may freeze my lungs." Studies in both humans and dogs indicate cold damage to the respiratory tract and lung tissue to be extremely rare. Scientific experiments in resting men and dogs have determined that breathing air temperatures from -25 degrees to -212 degrees respectively, were heated to well above freezing temperatures (75 degrees) before reaching the bronchi. Breathing cold air, therefore is unlikely to cause cell destruction in the respiratory tract. The uncomfortable sensations sometimes experienced in the airways are more likely associated with the customary dryness of cold air rather than the temperature. Dryness may irritate the upper airways in much the same way as training in a heated, dry indoor track facility in wintertime.

Cold may encourage angina in cardiac patients or bronchial hyper-reactivity in asthmastics. In general, these individuals can be encouraged to continue outdoor training in the winter. Because of the specific nature of cardiac and respiratory disorders, these persons should proceed only after consultation with and supervision by their personal physician.

Despite the potential dangers of cold the thermo-regulatory system is still more concerned with facilitating heat dissipation rather than heat conservation. Energy expenditures during running commonly average between 56 to 75 percent of our maximal exercise (aerobic) capacity, generating from 12 to 16 times the rate of heat production at rest. Encapsulation by a relatively thin 70 degree layer of warm air at the skin surface necessitates considerable sweating and evaporative heat loss to dissipate these large thermal loads. Clothing should be selected that will afford adequate protection against chilling at lower running speeds. Yet the same clothing should promote heat loss through sweat evaporation at higher energy expenditures.

Air is a superb insulator and lightweight, porous absorbent materials will usually provide acceptable protection under most cold conditions. When starting out, a thin layer of trapped air helps prevent loss of body heat. As the runner warms up and heat dissipating mechanisms are called upon, the wicking action of the porous clothing promotes sweat transfer to the outer garments where maximum evaporation can occur.

Adequate protective covering is best described in terms of the standard "clo" unit which is approximately equivalent to the insulation provided by the clothing you usually wear to maintain comfort at room temperature (70 degrees). The figure shows how dramatically clo unit requirements are reduced when going from a resting to exercise state. For example, the 7.75 clo units required at rest at 0 degrees are reduced to approximately 1 clo unit when running 7.5 to 10.5 mph. Even as temperatures become lower and insulation needs do not appreciably increase, it is important to recognize that slower running speeds will require added protection.

The windchill factor is also critical at low temperatures. Windchill expresses the relative discomfort associated with the combined effects of absolute temperature and wind velocity. This "effective" temperature is a more appropriate indicator of clo unit requirements. Charts are available, but weather forecasts on the radio provide the most convenient and current local chill-factor readings. Windchill has a dramatic effect on absolute temperatures; for example, a 10 mph wind at 0 degrees would reduce effective temperature to -40 degrees. Severe cold, such as this, is capable of freezing exposed flesh within minutes. Also, a runner's own speed generates a chill factor equivalent to the pace resulting in an additive effect when directly confronting a headwind. A pace of 9 mph directly into a 5 mph headwind is equivalent to a 14 mph wind speed. (See the chart entitled "Insulating Requirements At Different Energy Expenditures in the Cold" at the end of this chapter.)

I experience adequate cold protection when training between -25 degrees to -35 degrees effective temperature wearing cotton underwear, lined support, nylon shorts, heavy T-shirt, hooded cotton sweat suit, nylon top, leather ski mittens and goggles, heavy socks, and leather or nylon shoes. Nylon is very effective in its windproofing qualities and is particularly adept at minimizing the variable chill factor associated with fluctuating air currents. Admittedly, sweat evaporation is somewhat reduced. But I remove the lightweight top and tie it around my waist when I become uncomfortably warm.

Successful adjustments to cold weather training can be accomplished according to the following summary of principles and practices.

1. When running at customary training intensities between 7.5 and 10.5 mph, the body will be more concerned with heat elimination than heat retention, even if the outdoor temperatures are very low.

2. Lightweight porous clothing will provide sufficient warmth comfort to protect against chilling. Yet this clothing will facilitate sweat evaporation at the surface. Garments containing high percentages of cotton and/or wool are preferable to tightly woven impervious materials.

3. The amount of clothing (clo units) will vary somewhat according to prevailing weather conditions. Always dress for the most severe chill factor.

4. Other compensatory adjustments that will promote warmth comfort include wearing a nylon top for improved windchill protection and wearing facial protection when there is danger of frostbite (-40 degrees including windchill). In this regard, well ventilated ski goggles provide excellent protection of the upper face and forehead. Lower facial coverings should minimize restrictions to breathing. A "sheik like" veil of terry cloth, draped across the face bridging the nose and fastened to the head cover at ear level, provides both a wind screen and thermal protection and does not impede breathing. Frost or ice condensation is not a problem.

Start out with prevailing winds, if possible. This is contrary to the opinion of many who contend that it is preferable to begin against the wind so as to have it at your back on the way home. Several personal misfortunes have convinced me that frostbite occurs most often during the early phase of a workout. During the first few minutes of the run, cold sensations from the face (numbness, stiffness, burning) appear to underestimate actual conditions. The first few minutes are ample time for tissue freezing at frostbite threshold temperatures. Unfortunately, you become unpleasantly aware of them sometime later. To permit increased time for my cold receptors to translate the problem I routinely start running with the wind in more severe conditions.

Run in areas which afford a maximum of shelterbelt protection in severe weather. The interruption of wind speeds by trees, buildings, hills, gullies, etc., can really modify the chill factor effect.

Running A Marathon In The Cold

Not many marathons are held in below-freezing temperatures. Yet often, in early spring or late fall when relatively cold (25 to 45 degree) windy, wet weather is encountered, exposed tissues may experience uncomfortable localized cooling of the minimally clad runner despite high rates of energy expenditures. The knees and thighs seem especially vulnerable to chilling by convective air currents. It is distressing when these tissues stiffen up with normal fatigue without the added effects of numbing cold sensations. Knowing the course route, prevailing wind direction and velocities will enable you to approximate how long you may have to confront wind and rain directly.

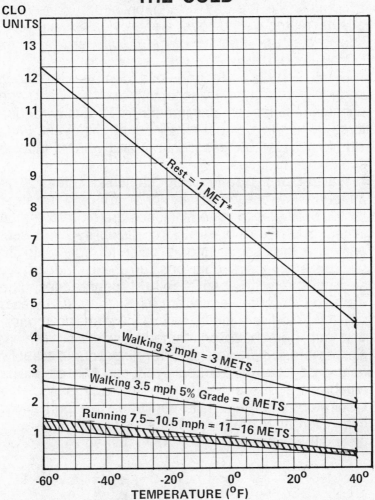

INSULATING REQUIREMENTS AT DIFFERENT ENERGY EXPENDITURES IN THE COLD

CLO UNITS

Rest = 1 MET*

Walking 3 mph = 3 METS

Walking 3.5 mph 5% Grade = 6 METS

Running 7.5–10.5 mph = 11–16 METS

TEMPERATURE (°F)

*MET refers to the metabolic rate or heat production of a resting man.

Informed estimation is always superior to guesstimation in the selection of the most suitable dress for prevailing conditions. An effective compromise to accommodate the understandably strong preference against restrictive leg cover and provide some protection is a liberal coating of petroleum jelly.

You should also—

Drink Fluids: Although less demand is placed upon the sweating mechanism in the cold, the drinking of fluids remains important. That may require force-drinking when not thirsty during the event. Fluid stops may also be less frequent and volume intakes somewhat reduced.

Warm-Up Properly: Pay particular attention to adequate warm-up activity prior to cold weather races. Muscular-tendinous injuries are more common in the cold. Passive stretching, flexibility exercises, easy running, some striding out, etc., for 15 to 20 minutes pre-race should position the runner at the starting line with about 0.5 to 1 degree desirable elevation in core temperature. Shed your sweats about four to five minutes before the start (no sooner) and put them back on immediately after finishing. Remember, when you stop running your metabolic heat production is markedly reduced. An athlete is much more susceptible to chilling and associated respiratory disorders if he continues to stand about thinly clad after the race. Don sweats and preferably go indoors to a warm, dry environment.

Alan D. Claremont is a physiologist at The University of Wisconsin, Madison.

Dealing With Pain

by Charles T. Kuntzleman

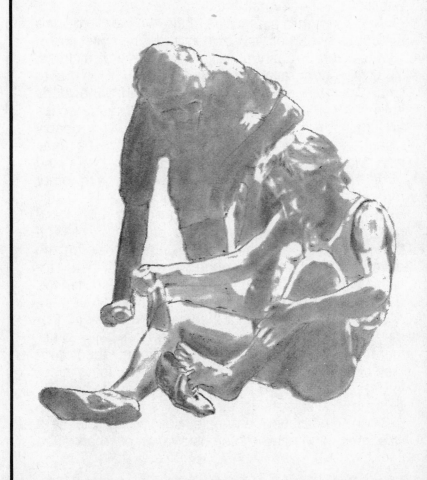

Can you expect to suffer severe aches and pains when you take up marathon training? Not if you follow the advice in this book and approach marathoning in a safe and sane manner.

Of course, pain is a private matter. We all respond differently to it. For some of us the idea of a pin prick is catastrophic and for others it is no big deal. Our response to pain is predicated on many factors. What may be significant pain for one person may be just another twinge for another.

So as you train, and continue to train, you will undoubtedly gather your own little private collection of twinges, throbs, aches, pains, and general distress. You will suffer ailments that lead you to discover "muscles you did not even know you had," and "body noises" completely new to you. Most of these aches and pains will not be important and will probably disappear. Those that worsen will have to be dealt with. Many ailments will be relieved through trial and error and some through conversations with other runners. A few may require medical attention.

However unique or common your body noises and pains turn out to be, you are the best judge of what they mean. So pay attention to them. Draw on the experiences of others whenever you can to understand your own afflictions. There are certain general guidelines for preventing or at least limiting your pain, and we'll be talking about them later on. They may or may not work for you. Get together with other marathoners and runners and ask them about pain they have been having and what they are doing about it. Try out things you think might work. If the pain persists, try something else.

Often the solution is simple, but finding it takes a little imagination and close observation of what you're

One way to eliminate continuing pain in the knee is to switch the direction of your run.

doing. Dr. George Sheehan, the long distance runner's guru, for example, found that one way to eliminate a continuing pain in his left knee was to switch the direction of his run. He had a habit of running with the flow of traffic along the road. After putting up with the pain for a while he decided to try to run against the flow of traffic, and the pain went away. The cause was not physiological, nor the solution magical. It was simply the slant of the road that had gradually created an imbalance in his running style and a strain on his left knee. Had he been running on a banked indoor track or on a beach, both the problem and the solution would have been the same.

Take comfort, then. Here you have Sheehan, an expert, working out problems with pain just like the rest of us. Occupational hazards are shared by veteran and novice alike. Everyone will go through pain, more or less.

Prevention

Most of the aches and pains in long distance running come from the skeleton and muscles.

Keeping pain to a minimum requires that you do three essential things.

1. Take good care of your feet.
2. Strengthen the muscles, ligaments, tendons, joints of your feet, legs, and abdomen.
3. Develop flexibility in your body's muscular and skeletal systems.

Care Of The Feet

It shouldn't be surprising that care of the feet head the

list. They take the most direct shocks as they propel you over all kinds of surfaces. The 52 oddly shaped bones crunched together inside a couple of little skin bags are really rather wonderful.

They take the most punishment, so caring for them is the single most important thing a marathoner can do to prevent or alleviate stress. By trial and error, scientific investigation, and by talking to other runners, experts have discovered that improper care can cause pain in the knees and legs as well as the feet.

Take a good look at your running shoes. With your socks they are the only protection your feet have as they continually beat against the running surface. Do they fit properly? Does your foot squish around or rub against the inside, even a little? Or, is there too little room? Are the shoes laced tightly enough? Or, do they cut off circulation?

Socks that are too thick, slow the blood's circulation if they make your feet, in effect, too large for the shoes you are using. Thin socks, on the other hand, cannot give your feet the cushions they need. Thick or thin, your socks should fit your foot, so they don't bunch up inside your shoes to create irritation and blisters.

Once the runner starts to feel little irritations on his feet, however minor they may be, he automatically reacts to them. Unconsciously, he favors this or that until he abandons his natural running style altogether. As a consequence, he introduces stresses that weren't there before and which generate pains else-where in the body.

Strengthen Your Muscles

To avoid pain, you must also strengthen your muscles and ligaments, the tendons of your feet and legs, and your abdomen. Of course, your muscles, ligaments, joints, and tendons are automatically conditioned as you run. But, you may need to do more. Some muscles are not as active as they should be. These include the muscles on the front of your calf, on the front of your lower leg, and in your abdomen. You will have to do specific exercises to compensate. If all of these muscles are conditioned properly, pain will be reduced.

Your abdominal muscles do not receive adequate stimulation when running. Consequently, exercises such as sit-ups, V-seats, curl ups, and look ups must be used to condition these muscles. Below are a series of recommended exercises for you. You should do three or four of these exercises each day. Start out with about five repetitions and eventually build up to 30. These exercises will overcome the problems associated with a lack of conditioning.

RECOMMENDED EXERCISES

Sit-Ups

1. Lie on your back with your knees bent and arms across your chest. You may also extend your arms along your sides or over your head, or place your hands behind your neck.
2. Curl your body up into a sitting position by first drawing your upper body off the floor. Keep your back rounded throughout the movement.

STEP 2

Look-Up/Curl-Down
1. Lie on your back, your lower back area touching the floor, knees bent.
2. Curl your head and upper body upward and forward to about a 45° angle. (Be sure you curl up; don't jerk and don't arch your back.)
3. Hold briefly and return to the starting position.
4. Repeat several times, then proceed with the Curl-Down/Look-Up exercise.

STEP 2

Curl-Down/Look-Up

1. Sit on the floor with your knees bent and your hands behind your head.
2. Slowly lower your upper body downward to a 45° angle or until you feel your stomach muscles begin to pull.
3. Hold briefly, then return to starting position.
4. Repeat several times.

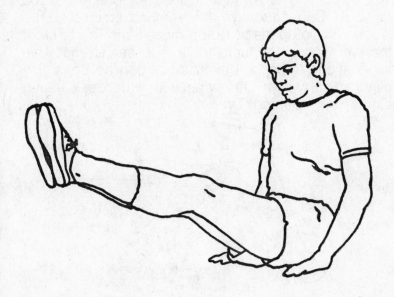

STEP 2

V-Seat

1. Sit on the floor with your legs extended and your hands on the floor next to your hips.

2. Slowly raise your legs off the floor and tilt your upper body backward slightly. Your body should form a V. (Keep your back slightly rounded.)

3. Hold for three to six seconds. (A more difficult variation is to describe a figure eight with your feet.)

4. Return to starting position. Repeat several times.

Another area of your anatomy that is not adequately affected by running are the muscles of the front of your leg. The shin muscles are used primarily for stabilization of the leg. They're not used for propelling you forward. Consequently, these muscles tend to be weaker in comparison to the muscles in the back of the leg. To compensate for this lesser strength we suggest the knee curl exercise. It can be done any place and any time. Do it when sitting at a desk, eating dinner, or watching TV.

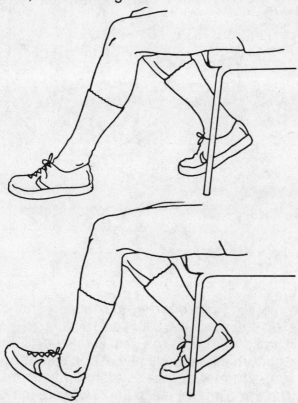

While seated, extend one leg. Lift toes while keeping heel on the floor. Repeat with other leg.

Developing Flexibility

It is also crucial that you develop flexibility in your muscular and skeletal systems. Pay particular attention to the muscles and tendons on the back of the legs. Running causes them to shorten.

Therefore, we recommend that you do the exercises on p58-76. Do these exercises slowly. They will help prevent leg pain and reduce the chances of injury. Some people call these exercises "joint-readiness preparation." The series will stretch your muscles and tendons and prevent problems common to most runners.

Normal Complaints, Aches, Pains And What To Do About Them.

Anyone who takes up running seriously will have to endure one or more of the aches and pains we'll be talking about. The most superbly conditioned runner may not be entirely free of them. So let's start from the ground up.

The Toes

Most of the stress felt in the toes comes from running shoes that fit poorly. Therefore, when trying on a new pair of running shoes, be sure they fit well in the toe section. Shoe widths are measured across the widest part of the foot sole. Occasionally the shoes taper too drastically in the toe area. So be careful. Other brands may be too wide here for your particular foot. Make sure the fit is right for you. The size of your running shoe does not indicate the fit you can expect for your foot. The shape of your foot finally determines the shoe you should choose for maximum comfort. So select a design that matches your foot as closely as possible.

Few things are more aggravating to a runner than toenails that cut into the flesh of the toes every time the foot hits the ground. The solution is as simple as the problem is painful. Keep your toenails trimmed, especially the corners.

In the foot's longest bone, the metatarsal, the stress of running can produce fractures so small they may not even be visible on an x-ray. Normally they would not have to be splinted or put into a cast. They simply would heal by themselves. But this takes time, maybe a month or two, even if you do not subject them to severe strain. That will probably mean that you must delay your marathon training program while they heal. It doesn't mean you'll have to stop your running program, however. During this time you would be wise to run on very soft surfaces at a reduced pace for shorter distances.

Morton's Foot

Morton's foot is not a disease, but a matter of bone structure. Normally, the big toe is the longest. But with the classic Morton's foot, the first metatarsal bone is short. The result is that the second toe is longer than the first. With this condition, normal balance is disturbed and the weight stress falls toward the inside arch. Although many people do not experience difficulties, others develop a callus in this area. There are also additional stresses and strains on the foot and leg.

Usually they can be corrected by wearing a special insert called an orthodic. Those with Morton's foot should look for shoes with roomy toe areas that permit the foot to slide forward without too much pressure on the ends of the toes. If you have foot pain and a Morton's foot, we recommend that you see a podiatrist.

Blisters

Blisters are a common ailment. Regardless of the type of shoe worn and the protective measures taken, foot blisters continue to plague many people. But they become a major problem only when they are severe enough to affect the quantity and quality of running. Problems also occur when infection develops.

Foot blisters are caused by heat. They are really burns produced by friction. The best way to prevent blisters is to stop the friction that causes them.

Here are some recommendations.

1. Buy high quality shoes and make sure they fit properly.
2. Take good care of your shoes. Don't allow them to get brittle so that hot spots develop.
3. Do not wear a new shoe to run a considerable distance. It is a good idea to wear new shoes around the house for a few minutes each day. As they begin to soften, wear them for running short distances (10 to 20 minutes). Then you can move up to longer distances.
4. Wear socks to help prevent blisters. The socks should be clean and snug fitting.

When a blister does develop, you want to prevent infection. To do this, keep the area clean. Do not puncture small blisters immediately. If you do puncture a blister once it has gotten larger, do so with a sterile needle to release the fluid, squeezing gently with sterile gauze.

Do not remove the skin. Place a pad of gauze and possibly foam rubber over the open blister. Next, continue to run if you can do so without significant pain. Consult your physician or podiatrist at the first sign of infection or complication.

Runner's Heel

This is a term used for a group of heel problems that include bone bruises and heel spurs—painful bony growths on the heel bone itself. These ailments are normally caused by running on a hard surface, stepping on sharp objects with force enough to cause a bruise, or wearing poorly designed running shoes. These complaints don't lend themselves to a quick cure. Rest is good for them, but not always desirable for those who want to maintain their conditioning.

A far better treatment is a heel "donut," a foam pad with a hole cut in the middle. The foam pad is then placed over the bone spur with the sensitive spot protruding through the hole. The donut is taped to your foot. We've known many runners who have had heel bruises so severe that doctors recommended surgery. Many tried the donut before making the final decision on surgery, and in a matter of weeks were painfree. It's simple therapy, but effective.

The Achilles Tendon

The Achilles tendon is a thick tendon at the back of the leg that connects the heel and foot to the back of the calf muscles. It controls the hinge-like action of the ankle with every running step and therefore does a lot of work during a run.

Achilles tendon injuries are debilitating. They not only stop you from running but keep you from running for a long time. It has been said that once you have an Achilles problem you'll always have one.

Sports medicine experts have identified three types of problems with the Achilles tendon. The first is tendonitis, an inflammation of the tendon. The second is a partial rupture, a tearing of the tendon fibers. And the third is a complete rupture or a complete break of the tendon itself. The last two are not common to most runners.

Tendonitis, however, is quite common. Usually, it is caused by a sudden change in routine. For example, you may change shoes, or run on grass and then switch to cinders, or go from one type of training to another. Symptoms of tendonitis are pain and stiffness an hour or so following activity, slight swelling, pain on contracting and streching of the calf muscle, and tenderness when squeezing pressure is applied at the tendon's narrowest point. Running becomes very difficult and springing practically impossible.

Tendons also become inflamed and swollen when they are constricted by equipment. If you feel pain in your Achilles tendon, your running shoes could be the culprit. The heels may be too low or too hard, or the backs too tight, putting a strain on the tendon or crowding it. Perhaps the arch support in the shoes is not adequate.

Tendonitis can also be caused by years of wearing heeled shoes. The heels favored by Americans shorten the Achilles tendons and make them less resilient. Often, the tendons tighten from running. That is why stretching exercises are so important to the runner. They limber up the tendons and counter-act the effects of running and the wearing of heels.

Self-treatment of tendonitis can be summarized in a few sentences. If it hurts you, put cold water or ice on the injured area. If there is pain, reduce your activity to a point where you can tolerate the pain. Slow down or stop, if the pain gets worse while exercising. In simple terms, if you're not hurting, you probably aren't hurting yourself.

When you first injure your Achilles, stretching should be avoided at all costs—overstretching led to the problem in the first place. Also, wear well-heeled shoes and run on flat, smooth, straight surfaces. Do not do any fast running. As long as there is tendon inflammation and pain, ice or cold water after each running session may be helpful. This does not really cure the injury—it simply helps you endure the pain.

To prevent Achilles tendonitis from developing, do plenty of stretching in your warm-up. The cause of tendon injuries appears to be shortness and inflexibil-ity. This is usually because we always wear shoes with substantial heels. Suggested stretching exer-cises include standing on the heels of the feet, drawing the toes up as far as possible, or putting your toes on a two-inch board and stretching the heel downward. Avoid sudden and violent changes in routine—running on the level, for example, and then suddenly changing to running on hills. Or, running on a track and then suddenly switching to a road, or running short distances and then suddenly running long distances.

Shin Splints

Shin splints are a pain on the forefront of the shin. If you have a shin splint you will feel pain in the lower leg

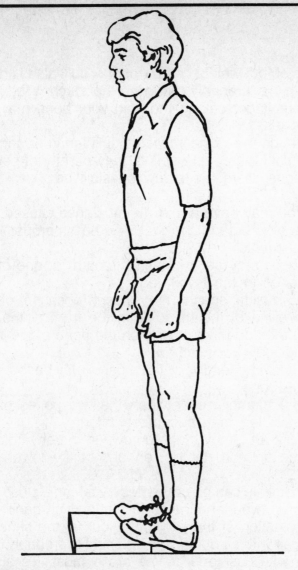

STEP 1

Achilles Stretch

1. Stand with balls of feet on a 1- to 2-inch block of wood (or a book); heels on floor.

2. Hold in this position for several seconds.

when you put weight on your foot. You'll also find that your shin is probably tender to the touch. When you run your fingers along the shin your bone may feel roughened.

Although the name implies a splintering or damage to the shin bone, shin splints may be any of several conditions. Here are a few possibilities.

1. You may have a muscle imbalance caused by a "toeing out" of the feet or other improper body mechanics.
2. There may be a hair-line fracture of one of the bones in the lower leg.
3. A muscle spasm may occur because of the swelling of the muscles in the front of the leg.
4. The tendon that inserts on the bone of the lower leg may be inflamed.
5. The same tendon or the muscle may be torn from the bone.
6. The membrane between the two bones of the lower leg may become irritated.
7. Your arch may drop somewhat, thereby irritating one or more of the tendons of the lower leg.

Shin splints can be prevented by taking a close look at your footwear and the surfaces. In all probability it's a combination of the two. Let's look at the shoes. A good pair with a rippled sole and heel is probably best. Shoes with cushioned soles are a must. It's also a good idea to have a shoe with a lower heel. You should also consider switching from a hard to a soft running surface whenever possible. A golf course or a local park offers the runner a chance to work out on grass which is much softer than pavement or a track. Another thing you might try to do is reverse the

Avoid sudden changes in routine. Don't run on a track and switch to grass.

direction of your running on a track. Instead of always going counterclockwise, switch back and forth so you do not place a great deal of stress on the inside of the leg as you go around the turns.

Also try to avoid running on your toes. This practice sometimes causes shin splints. Put a sponge heel pad in the heel section of your shoe to help absorb some of the stress from running on harder surfaces. You can also try placing a molded crest under the toes.

To prevent shin splints from occurring, it's a good idea to condition the muscles in the front of the leg. Running does a great deal to strengthen the muscles in the back of the leg. A muscle imbalance occurs. The muscles in the back of the leg are a lot stronger than the ones in the front. This sets you up for shin splints. To compensate for that you'll want to strengthen the muscles in the front. The foot flexor with weights or an isometric exercise is a good idea. Here you flex your foot up and down against resistance. If you have no weights to strap on, sit with your legs dangling, feet not touching the floor, and have a friend hold your feet while you're trying to lift them. Do this for 3 sets of 10 each day. If you don't have shin splints now, you can do this exercise to help prevent them from occurring.

The Knee

The knee, the largest and most complicated joint of the body, is a true hinge joint. The two main bones of the joint are the thigh and shin bones. The convex surfaces of the thigh bone fit into the concave surfaces of the shin bone. These bones serve as a place of attachment for the muscles and ligaments. The bones, muscles and ligaments permit efficient movement and support of the joint.

Thirteen separate ligaments and tendons provide most of the support for the knee. Lateral stability is maintained by the internal and external lateral ligaments. The cross-shaped ligaments keep the thigh bone from sliding forward and backward on the shin bone.

The entire joint is enclosed in a sac forming the joint capsule. The sac contains bursae which secrete a lubricating fluid during joint motion. Situated on the top of the shin bone are small cartilages, or menisci. They are constructed of tough fibrous tissue. Their function is to cushion and absorb shock between the thigh and shin bone.

The knee flexes and extends, rotates inward and outward, with the assistance of connected organs. The flexion of the knee occurs because of the contraction of the muscle at the back of the leg, called the hamstrings. The extension is caused by the muscles in the front of the upper leg called the quadriceps femoris.

The knee, though the largest joint in the body, is vulnerable to injuries. Its main support comes from tissue, so it has very little defense against a blow from the side. Injuries to the knee joint are incapacitating, and in some instances, keep you from participating in athletics—especially contact sports.

The muscles located above and below the knee aid in stability. Conditioned properly, they will help protect the knee from injuries. Knee exercises can do this job well. Traditionally, deep knee bends, full squats, and duck walks were used to condition the muscles of the legs. Recent investigations, however, have revealed that these exercises do more harm than good. In fact, these exercises may make people more susceptible to injuries because they are potentially dangerous to the internal and supporting structures of the knee joint and place great stress on the ligaments and cartilage.

Your knee, despite its vulnerability, can stand a remarkable degree of stress and still work pretty well. That it can survive even one brutal crush by several 250-pound professional football players hitting it from different angles, strains our belief. But that happens, thousands of times, every football season. Fortunately, runners like us do not have to sacrifice our knees for the glory of pro football. Still, on your run through the neighborhood or along the beach, your knees are not completely safe from stress. Usually, pains are associated with the kneecap, beneath it or along its sides. Sometimes, the kneecap does not articulate smoothly against the lower end of the thighbone as it should, and the knee becomes increasingly irritated and swollen as you run. If you have this problem, you may have to curtail your running program. But first, experiment with different running methods, because a lot of doctors think this problem may be caused, or aggravated, by the way your foot strikes the ground. Earlier, we mentioned Dr. Sheehan who learned to switch directions as he ran along a sloping road or on a banked track. By doing this, he compensated for unnatural stresses that were creating a knee problem. If you run indoors on a banked tracked in one direction for long distances, your knees may be headed for trouble. Even a subtle slope such as that on a banked road or on a beach may also cause problems. So beware.

Muscle Cramps And Spasms

When one of your muscles contracts powerfully and painfully, you have a muscle cramp. The contraction may occur at any time—at rest as well as during activity. Cramps usually occur without warning. Occasionally, however, you may be able to feel one "building up."

There are a number of causes for muscle cramps. They include fatigue; cold; imbalance of salt, potassium, and water levels; a sharp blow; or overstretching of unconditioned muscles.

You can probably reduce the chances of a cramp by maintaining a proper diet, making sure you have a proper warm-up prior to vigorous activity, and stopping activity before you become extremely fatigued. Tapering off is a good idea.

Once a cramp does occur, it can usually be stopped by simply stretching the muscle affected and firmly kneading it. Usually, a sense of tightness or dull pain will follow, making it necessary to apply heat and massage to the area to restore circulation.

If you're plagued with frequent cramps, you can usually eliminate the problem by drinking plenty of fluids, eating foods high in salt and potassium, and doing muscle strengthening and stretching exercises.

Sprains And Strains

While cramps and spasms are essentially painful contractions of muscle tissue, a strain is something else. A strain is an overstretching, or even a tearing of a muscle or tendon. A sprain on the other hand is when a ligament is stretched or torn. Small blood vessels in the area break and pain develops when the surrounding tissue swells up and overstimulates sensitive nerve endings.

Because the ankle becomes such a vulnerable pivot when you are running, ankle strains and sprains occur. Obviously, you should watch where you are going. That means you should be careful where you run. You should, at least, learn how to pick your way among the potholes and sidestep any beer cans that may be littering your path.

If you aren't very good at this and manage to sprain or strain an ankle, you will have to postpone further running until it is healed.

Muscle Soreness And Stiffness

Even those who have been running for years some-times complain of sore and stiff muscles. The pain may occur immediately following the activity, or after some delay, usually 24 to 48 hours. Often the discomfort lasts for only a few days, though after periods of severe exercise, it may last for a week. Muscles most commonly affected are the calves and the front and back muscles of the thigh.

Medical authorities have been unable to say conclusively what causes soreness and stiffness. The pain during and immediately after exercise is probably due to waste products which are formed during exercise and remain in the fluid surrounding the cells. And when stiffness occurs approximately 24 to 48 hours after exercise, it may be the result of small muscle tears or localized contractions of muscles.

To completely avoid muscle soreness and stiffness is practically impossible. But you can reduce the intensity by planning your conditioning program so that you progress gradually, especially during the beginning stages. That approach will allow the muscles of the body to adapt themselves to the work they must do.

If you become sore and stiff from physical activity,

some additional light exercises or general activity often provides temporary relief, though the pain usually returns when you stop. Tapering-off will mitigate such undesirable after-effects. So will massage.

Side Stitch

The side stitch, like shin splints, is a common affliction among runners, especially during the first stages of conditioning. The pain is sharp and usually makes itself felt just under the rib cage. The side stitch is probably the result of two basic causes.

The first is improper breathing. This creates spasms in the diaphragm. To reduce the problem, do "belly breathing." That is, when you inhale, distend the diaphragm, pushing the abdominal wall out. When you exhale, push the diaphragm in so the belly is flattened. It's just the reverse of what you would normally do.

The second cause is probably the most common. It's a spasm of the ligaments attached to the liver, pancreas, stomach, and intestines. These ligaments are put under stress when you run vigorously. The bouncing action causes them to stretch, causing the pain. You can end the side stitch by simply gripping the side and pushing it in. In severe cases, you can lie on your back and raise your feet in the air, or even try standing on your head or hands. The inverted position relaxes the ligaments and relieves the spasm.

There are some other things you can try with the side stitch. Don't eat or drink within three hours before running; during the attack, bend forward, inhale deeply, and push the belly out; and if the pain is intolerable, lie flat on your back, raise your legs over your head, and support your hips.

The side stitch is a common affliction during the first stages of conditioning.

Serious Aches And Pains

Back Pains

Back pains should not be fooled with, particularly if they occur in the lower back. Low back pain can signal a slipped spinal disc. Obviously, back problems cannot be diagnosed on the running path, but if you have a slipped disc, you'll know it and fast.

Some lower back pains result from exercising after years of relative inactivity. You will have to guess at the seriousness of these pains by the way you feel at the time; that is, how intense they are, and how much they limit your activity. In any case, go slowly. Feel your way. If for any reason you think further exercise might cause any harm, discontinue running and consult your physician about the pain.

We have some notions about the causes of back pain. Usually, it is the result of poor posture and poor fitness.

Improper sitting posture can lead to low back problems. As in lifting, the back should be kept erect. To sit slouched in a chair puts unnecessary tension on the back muscles. Poorly designed furniture, which is constructed without regard for body structure, can cause strain, fatigue, and pain in muscles. Sitting for prolonged periods causes shortening of certain postural muscles, particularly the hamstrings. If you are involved in an occupation which requires you to sit for prolonged periods, you must practice stretching exercises regularly to maintain hamstring muscles at their proper length.

A bed that is too soft or sags in the middle is the worst enemy of any back. No matter what posture you assume on such a bed, muscles are subjected to constant tension. At a time when the muscles should be completely relaxed, many of them are placed under stress throughout the night. It is no wonder that these muscles, the spinal erectors being the ones most often affected, are sore in the morning. Many physicians suggest the use of a board under the mattress to alleviate the condition.

But the real problem lies in poor fitness, specifically, weak abdominals. At the pelvis, the weight of the upper body is transferred to the lower limbs. The pelvis, or pelvic girdle, is balanced on the rounded heads of the thigh bones. To the pelvis are attached numerous muscles which hold it in place.

Some of the muscles involved are the abdominals, hamstrings, gluteals, and hip flexors.

Any imbalance or weakness in those muscles can lead to pelvic misalignment, which usually manifests itself as a forward or backward tilt of the pelvis.

If the abdominal muscles which attach to the front of the pelvis and hold it up are weak, the top of the pelvis will drop down and tilt forward. The sacrum (just below the spine) also tilts forward, putting increased tension on the sacroiliac joint and the ligaments located on the front of the lumbar vertebrae. Forward tilt of the pelvis leads to lordosis, or sway back. It is in that situation that the "slipped disc" injury most often occurs.

In addition to abdominal weakness, a lack of strength in the gluteals and/or hamstrings can also lead to forward pelvic tilt. While the abdominals stabilize the pelvis by pulling upward on the front, the gluteals and hamstrings contribute to stability by pulling down on the rear of the pelvis.

Exercises must be done to strengthen the abdominals and gluteals. Usually the running does it for the gluteals. But the abdominal muscles must be conditioned with special exercises, such as those listed in "The Preparation Plan" section of this book.

Quite a few runners have found that their back pain disappeared after this kind of exercise program. That is, running and abdominal exercises. We are not promoting any miracle cures. On the contrary, we urge you to be extremely cautious. If you have back trouble and do not approach running with common sense and care, you can make the condition worse.

Dizziness

Dizziness is another warning sign to which you should respond without hesitation. It can indicate the early stages of heat exhaustion or heat stroke, especially if you are running in hot weather and the humidity is high. Even if it is neither hot nor humid, dizziness can be cause for alarm; when it is accompanied by shortness of breath, it may signify the presence of circulatory difficulties or other problems of major medical significance.

If you experience any of these symptoms, stop until they go away, then begin to jog again very slowly. In most cases the discomfort will be momentary and no cause for worry. It will disappear as quickly as it came. But if it recurs as you continue to exercise, stop running altogether and see your doctor.

Heart Problems

Be particularly wary of extreme and/or persistent pains in the arms, chest, neck, head, ears, or upper abdomen. One physician known to us, cites the case of an internist who, curiously, suffered with such pains for an entire day before he gave in to them and decided he'd better get help. It was a heart attack, to no one's surprise but his, but he was lucky enough to survive.

If you experience any of these pains, we strongly suggest that you not be as thick-headed as he was. The symptoms of an attack can take different forms: a very heavy pressure, as if someone were sitting on top of your chest; an extreme tightness inside the center of your chest, like a clenched fist; a feeling something like indigestion; a stuffiness high in your stomach or low in your throat. Whenever you have a strong symptom that even closely resembles any one of these, stop running at once and get to a physician.

You may have gone through a stress ECG before you started a running program and passed it with flying colors. If so, your chance of having this experience is relatively small. But don't get cocky. Your body, not somebody else's electronic measurements, has the final word. So listen to it.

Charles T. Kuntzleman is a fitness consultant who put together Rating the Exercises and The Complete Book of Walking for CONSUMER GUIDE® magazine.

Mental
Toughness

by Charles T. Kuntzleman

Running a marathon takes a lot of mental toughness. Training for a marathon takes a lot of the same. If you want to be successful you must get your head together. Running a marathon is not something you decide to do one Saturday and then do seven days later.

Like any good thing, it takes time. You must spend months establishing those base miles and then upping the mileage three to six months prior to the run. The time commitment and the loneliness of this long distance running can get to you after a while—if you're not prepared for it.

To run a marathon requires adequate training and plenty of persistence. In fact, completing a marathon has more to do with persistence than it does with ability. And persistence is predicated on mental toughness.

Running one hour a day and devoting several minutes to an adequate warm-up and cool-down takes a real chunk of your time. In fact, it's over 6 percent of your total day and more than 8 percent of your time awake. At first that may not seem like much. You are probably already logging 20 or 30 minutes, three to four days a week. However, social, domestic, and job pressures can quickly undercut your best intentions. To stick to a schedule is difficult. But your goal is to run a marathon. You will have a lot of distractions. Don't let them interfere with you. You need a commitment to stick to a training regimen that will permit you to be successful.

The Mental Toughness Of Training

Some Sunday afternoon when everyone else is inside watching TV or curled up in front of a fire, you'll be out logging 13, 15, 17, or 20 miles. This long distance running will prepare you for your ultimate goal—the marathon. Sometimes you'll question your intelligence. You'll wonder if it's all worth it. Many of these runs will be done in solitude. The hills, the dogs, the stares, the pains, and the joys will be yours alone to experience. All this takes discipline. Unfortunately, there is no other way. If you expect to be successful in marathon running you'll need the mental toughness to continue running even though the lure to stay at home is great. It's on those days that your marathon character is built. For during the race you will experience a hellish pain. You may think that you will not be able to take another step. But the discipline learned in those training runs will pull you through. Because of the hard training you will know you will be able to finish because you did it before—under less than ideal conditions.

This suffering and mental toughness also teaches you a lot about yourself. You learn that you have powers you thought didn't exist. You learn that you are a hero because you have overcome incredible odds and won. Maybe you didn't participate in the Super Bowl, the World Series, or the World Cup; but you participated in a marathon and that, in itself, is a victory. You reached back and drew on your own resources to finish those miles in the heat, the cold, or the snow.

When the weather is cold and the wind is blowing and the wind chill factor is around -20 degrees, snow and ice will collect around your eyes, nose, and mouth. Your ears and hands will burn. At times, part of your body will be warm and other parts will be quite cold. The run on those days will be a real struggle. You'll want to quit. But you persist.

In the summer, the weather may be terribly hot. The humidity and temperature may make you want to stop. After a few miles, you feel exhausted. Again, you'll want to quit. But you hang in there and log your mileage—more mental toughness.

You'll be lonely. Practically every runner is. For some, this is mental toughness. But in time, you'll relish this loneliness. It will be a time for you to be alone in your thoughts, time to work out problems—personal, domestic, social, or business. It will be time to be away from the hassle of your workaday world. Time to be alone—growing, suffering, meditating.

After your longest run you'll announce to your spouse, co-workers, friends or children that you've reached a new high. You'll tell them you have covered X number of miles or minutes for the first time. You'll be met with stares of disbelief. Or stares of so what. And in a matter of seconds their stares will be again riveted to the TV, desk, sink, ironing board, or typewriter. They don't understand. They wonder why you do it. More mental toughness. One thing they can't take away from you, however, is the great feeling of accomplishment, the feeling that the time spent on the road was well worth it. You're proud of your accomplishment. You've become your own hero.

When this feeling of self-satisfaction and heroics dominates your thinking, and you no longer need to get strokes from other people for doing it, you can conclude that your self-discipline is starting to pay off. You're now internalizing the marathon drive. You know that what you're doing is going to pay off in what Bob Glover has called the "ultimate fitness challenge." You think that if you can finish this race you will have the strength to do anything. You feel as though you have found the fountain of youth.

Before you actually run a marathon, however, you must learn another lesson in mental toughness. As you train, and log the prescribed number of miles and hours, you will want to go further than what the charts

In the solitude of training, you can work out your problems.

tell you. That is very common. We advise that you overcome the temptation. Most of the time when you want to go further than the charts indicate, you're headed for trouble. Blisters, aches and pains, and other problems that we've talked about earlier are bound to come up. It takes a lot of discipline to stick to the regimen and program outlined. One week you may feel good and think that an extra 20 minutes a day won't hurt you. But the next week you will pay for it with a cold or ailment that will set your training program back. Staying with the charts takes patience.

Running The Marathon—
Mental Toughness

To run 26 miles takes chutspa. They called it guts in World War II. If you follow the CONSUMER GUIDE® plan you won't run 26 miles prior to the actual race. You'll probably run 3 hours or 20 miles. You'll need mental toughness to believe in yourself and our recommendations. You must believe you can run 26 miles even though you never did it in practice. The six extra miles in the marathon are difficult—no question about it. Those miles are going to take a lot of mental toughness on your part. Even though you haven't run 26 miles, you are ready. You will suffer. But everyone does. You'll need a lot of mental discipline and faith to know that the plan works.

The first part of mental toughness in running the marathon is before the race begins. You'll worry. You will have trained long and hard. It will take real mental toughness to tell yourself that this day is like any other day. You know it isn't, but you can try to talk yourself into it. If you can't, at least convince yourself to keep a cool head. Write down all the things you'll want to do.

For example, go to the bathroom, remember to take your running gear with you (shoes included), arrive on time, eat and drink properly.

At the race site you'll have more problems. You'll want to run to warm-up more than you should. You'll worry about the fact that you didn't sleep last night. You'll have all kinds of aches and pains. You'll seem edgy. You'll feel terribly nervous. Your stomach may hurt. You'll feel as though you won't be able to run more than a mile or two. These are all natural responses. If you let them get the best of you, you'll leave the race at the starting line. It takes mental toughness to control these urges and feelings before the race. It takes mental discipline to keep your head cool. Make sure, on the warm-up side of the run, that you don't run too far. For the marathon, walking is perhaps the best warm-up. Also, remember to do a lot of stretching. It's probably best to get to the race area about an hour to an hour and a half ahead of time. That will give you plenty of time to register, do your warm-ups, and get yourself in the proper frame of mind. You don't want to be rushed nor do you want to be bored. It takes a delicate balance.

Although this is a highly individual matter, it is best to remain alone in your warm-up. There is a natural tendency for you to want to be gregarious. But, talking to others takes your mind off the race. Thinking about the race is very important—athletes call it "psyching up." It is very important to reflect on what's going to happen in the race and how you're going to run it. Here again, it takes mental toughness not to be carried away with the crowd.

Even after the gun sounds you're going to need mental toughness. During the first few miles, you'll want to go faster than you should. Let's say you've been training at about an 8:30 pace. Now, because of the hoopla associated with the race start and the zest of competition, there's a tendency for you to go out at a 7:30 pace. You get caught up in the marathon frenzy. It takes real mental toughness to stay at your pre-determined pace. Consider the first five miles of

---

PACE CHART

This chart gives the average mile times for marathons from 2:10 (2 hours and 10 minutes) up to 5:00 hours. For example, a 4:20 marathon is 9 minutes and 55 seconds a mile.

2:10 = 4:57.5	3:26 = 7:51.4	3:50 = 8:46.4
2:15 = 5:08.9	3:27 = 7:53.7	3:51 = 8:48.6
2:20 = 5:20.4	3:28 = 7:56.0	3:52 = 8:50.9
2:25 = 5:31.8	3:29 = 7:58.3	3:53 = 8:53.2
2:30 = 5:43.3	3:30 = 8:00.6	3:54 = 8:55.5
2:35 = 5:54.7	3:31 = 8:02.9	3:55 = 8:57.8
2:40 = 6:06.2	3:32 = 8:05.2	3:56 = 9:00.1
2:45 = 6:17.6	3:33 = 8:07.4	3:57 = 9:02.4
2:50 = 6:29.0	3:34 = 8:09.7	3:58 = 9:04.7
2:55 = 6:40.5	3:35 = 8:12.0	3:59 = 9:06.9
3:00 = 6:51.9	3:36 = 8:14.3	4:00 = 9:09.2
3:05 = 7:03.4	3:37 = 8:16.6	4:05 = 9:20.7
3:10 = 7:14.8	3:38 = 8:18.9	4:10 = 9:32.1
3:15 = 7:26.3	3:39 = 8:21.2	4:15 = 9:43.6
3:16 = 7:28.5	3:40 = 8:23.5	4:20 = 9:55.0
3:17 = 7:30.8	3:41 = 8:25.8	4:25 = 10:06.5
3:18 = 7:33.1	3:42 = 8:28.0	4:30 = 10:17.9
3:19 = 7:35.4	3:43 = 8:30.3	4:35 = 10:20.2
3:20 = 7:37.7	3:44 = 8:32.6	4:40 = 10:22.5
3:21 = 7:39.9	3:45 = 8:34.9	4:45 = 10:24.8
3:22 = 7:42.3	3:46 = 8:37.2	4:50 = 10:27.1
3:23 = 7:44.6	3:47 = 8:39.6	4:55 = 10:29.4
3:24 = 7:46.8	3:48 = 8:14.9	5:00 = 10:31.7
3:25 = 7:49.1	3:49 = 8:44.2	

the run a warm-up. Don't forget it! If you do, you'll never finish the race. Don't let anyone tell you to do it any other way. If you're afraid you won't be able to hold the pace, it's best to find out who the experienced marathoners are and ask them what pace they're going to run at. If you find a runner who's going at your desired pace, it's best to settle right in behind him or her and stay there. Wear your watch, keep an eye on it, and make sure that you're staying at the pace you intended through those first few miles.

Between five and fifteen miles a new element of mental toughness becomes important. Aches and pains are bound to come up. You may start to worry. How significant is the pain? Will it affect your running later on in the race? Will the hip pain slow you down? Will it make you stop? Don't become obsessed with the pain but recognize it for what it is. You may be doing something incorrectly. Maybe you're running too much on the side of the road. Maybe you're running too hard. Concentrate on the problem. Probably the pain will go away. But it will give you the shakes for a while.

You'll also need discipline to stop or slow down and take a drink of liquid. We know there is a natural tendency for you to say: "Well, I'm going to finish this race no matter what. And I'm not going to stop running. The lack of water is not going to affect me." Don't kid yourself. Refusing to drink water is suicide. Replenishment of liquid at this particular time of the race is crucial. Although you may have to slow down to drink it, actually even walk, you may find that your pace picks up, simply because you replaced some of your fluid.

Of course, a few of you may be able to take a drink without stopping. It's pretty much an individual thing.

But if it's your first time it's probably best for you to slow down and actually walk. And you shouldn't be worried about stopping. Bill Rodgers, the first time he won the Boston Marathon and set a new U.S. record, stopped to drink liquids. He felt that he could not adequately replace his liquids while running. If the best marathoner in the United States can do it a beginner certainly can. Don't worry what others will say. Just have the mental discipline and toughness to stop and take the liquid. We guarantee you'll feel charged and ready for the next challenge.

Somewhere between 15 and 20 miles, more mental toughness is needed. You've been running for two hours or more. The run is getting long. Physically you may feel okay. But a general feeling of malaise may be setting in. And you're worried that you still have six to ten miles to go. Fatigue is starting to overtake you. You probably feel well enough to keep going. But you're concerned about the prospect of adding all those additional miles to your run. It is here that you learn a lot about your character. You learn patience. You learn something about your willpower. You learn you are not simply a spectator viewing an athletic contest, but an active participant.

At about 20 miles, you may hit "the wall." Up until this time you have run the first half of the race. The last six miles are the last half of the race. No matter what sport they have played—football, wrestling, basketball, track, or soccer, marathoners agree: "Never have I experienced pain like the last six miles in the marathon." We are not telling you this to scare you off. We're telling you this so that you're ready for it. When you hit the wall your legs will be hurting. Your muscles will ache. Fatique will seem so severe that you'll want to quit. Your mind will start to play tricks on you. You'll be angry, grumpy, and irritable. For you to continue to run during these last six miles will take more mental toughness and discipline than you've probably ever had. Almost any runner can cover 20 miles. But the last six miles are something else—the equivalent of 20 more.

During the last six miles you're going to find yourself

When you hit the "wall" you will only have run the first half of a marathon.

pushed to what seems to be your ultimate limit. You will need to call on all your resources—mental, physical, and spiritual. The last six miles take real courage. They will show you that you're able to endure a considerable amount of pain and survive.

Physiologists have not agreed on what the wall is. Some have said it is due to low blood sugar or the accumulation of lactic acid. Others have speculated that it may be due to dehydration or high body temperature. And still others have said that the wall is due to a loss of blood volume or a depletion of muscle glycogen. Most runners feel it's the latter. No one, however, really knows. But the wall is there for all of us.

One exercise physiologist, David Costill, Director of the Ball State University Human Performance Laboratory in Muncie, Indiana, ran a marathon because he wasn't sure that the wall existed. When he came to that point, however, he said: "The sensations of exhaustion were unlike anything I have ever experienced. I could not run, walk, or stand, and even found sitting a bit strenuous."

Marathon runners feel that the marathon is a microcosm of life. There's pain, joy, agony, and ecstasy. There is the challenge of doing something worth doing and then accomplishing it. Your success is contingent upon the work that went before.

It's the American work ethic personified. Work hard, stick to the task at hand, and be successful.

Charles T. Kuntzleman is a fitness consultant who put together Rating the Exercises *and* The Complete Book of Walking *for* CONSUMER GUIDE® *magazine.*

The Race
And How To
Run It

by Charles T. Kuntzleman

What follows is predicated on the assumption that you have followed our advice up to this point. That is, you have developed a good base mileage, followed our three to six months marathon training regimen, and listened to the wisdom of your body.

The First Time

The strategy of a marathon is simple. You start at the start, hang in the race at your pace, and finish at the finish. Of course, the race is difficult, but it is not a technical race. It can be completed with a lot of common sense. We don't want you to get swamped by the hoopla and mystique that surround the marathon. To help you we have set up 16 principles. These will guide you in the running of your first marathon.

Principle 1. Think in terms of completing a marathon. Not competing. It is crazy to run your first marathon with a thought to place highly. You'll be frustrated and disappointed. You have never run such a distance. To run 26 miles is in itself an important goal.

Principle 2. Set a realistic time goal. The goal should be based on your training runs. If you've been following the CONSUMER GUIDE® Training Program and running comfortably at an 8:30 pace for the last three months, a reasonable goal for you will be 3:40 to 3:45. Even here, however, you should not be a slave to the program. Your first and primary goal is to finish. The chart on page 148 shows you some reasonable goals based on your training pace.

Principle 3. Enter some shorter races. They will give you an opportunity to develop your pace, to feel the excitement of competition, and to learn more about running. These races can be any length but none should be more than 20 miles.

A course that has hills will take a lot out of you, even if there are a lot of downhills.

Principle 4. Pick an easy course. That is just plain common sense. Find a course that has few hills if any. A course that has hills will take a lot out of you, even if there are a lot of downhills. If you don't know the course, study the times of last year's event. If a large percentage of the times seem rather low, it is probably a fast course.

Principle 5. Choose a cool day. Heat can kill you. It can slow you down. Some experts have speculated that for every degree over 70 your pace is at least one to two minutes slower. That's for the better runners. For the novice it's probably a lot more. Worse, heat can really make your run miserable. We recognize that you can't choose the weather for the day. But you can make some reasonable judgments. You can determine normal temperature profiles. Try to select a run when the temperature is likely to be around 40 to 55 degrees. Also be careful of the other end of the extreme. Temperatures below 30 degrees can be uncomfortable. In the United States, March and April and October and November are probably the best times to run.

Principle 6. Try carbohydrate loading. Diet manipulation is not a must, but it may help you. We suggest that several weeks prior to a race or a long run, you try carbohydrate loading to see how your body handles the extra sugars and starches. But remember: everyone is different. This will be your experiment.

Principle 7. Check out the course before you run it. If possible drive your car around the course. You don't want to get lost. Usually this is not too much of a problem since you'll be near the middle or the back of the pack. But it does give you some confidence to know the course.

Principle 8. Wear a watch. The watch will help you with Principle 2. It will keep you from going out too fast. You can use it to check your progress. You may want to tape selected times to your wrist, that is, your time goals at 5, 10, 15, and 20 miles.

Principle 9. Find a friend or pacer. Before racing, try to find a runner who will be running at the same pace you want to. Pick a veteran. He or she will probably hold a steady pace. Run slightly behind and keep your eyes on this person. With so many entered in marathons these days, it should not be too difficult to find someone going at your speed. The pacer will aid you immensely in keeping you from going out too fast.

Principle 10. Decide that you're running for minutes rather than for seconds. Trying to make up 15 seconds for a drink of water is trouble. Bending over to tie your shoes for 30 seconds and then trying to make it up on the next mile is just going to affect your performance. The key to successful marathon running is a steady, steady pace. Some of the best marathoners in the world stop to drink or tie their shoes and think nothing of it. If they can do it so can you.

Principle 11. Start where you belong. If you have been training at an 8:30 pace and expect to run the marathon in roughly 3:45, put yourself with other runners who expect to run at the same pace. The start of marathons is staggered for runners of different abilities. Don't go up front with the group running it in 2:20 to 2:30. You should wait until your group is called. If you start too far in front you're going to be forced to run too fast in the beginning. If you go out too fast you'll falter at the end of the race. It's also unfair to run in front of faster runners. It affects their time adversely. Start where you belong.

Principle 12. Make sure you have helpers on the course. That is, people who can give you aid. They can give you extra clothing or hold the clothing you might want to discard. They can also give you water, time slips, petroleum jelly, bandages, moral support,

Helpers on the course can hold the clothing you might want to discard.

you name it. They are your guardian angels. They will give you the psychological lift you need. They are a breath of fresh air when the miles start to get you down.

Principle 13. Listen to your body. You are the best judge of you. You know when you are hurting. You know when you should back off, pick up the pace slightly, drink liquids, etc. The best marathoners in the world are highly conscious of what's happening to their bodies. If you see or feel something going wrong, you can do something about it. But if you're "spaced out" and completely mesmerized by the run, you can get into serious trouble before you realize it. And you'll probably have to terminate the race before reaching the end.

Principle 14. Do not charge hills. Although we told you to select a flat course you'll probably encounter a few hills. Sprinting or high stepping up hills is okay in training but not in the race. You want to get up that hill as easily and efficiently as possible. That means you are to run with the same effort as you used on level ground. The big boys and girls may win or lose a marathon in the hills but you're trying to complete a marathon, not compete. Don't forget that.

Principle 15. Take plenty of liquids. Never, never try to complete a marathon without taking on liquids. Drink water, beer—an athletic beverage like Gatorade or ERG, whatever you want. Just make certain that you do it. You can try to drink on the run. If you do, you'll probably get about one to two ounces and the rest down the front of you. And you'll probably lose a few seconds. You can also stop and take a good six to ten ounces and lose 15 to 20 seconds. That may seem like a big difference with respect to time but remember, this is a race of minutes, not seconds.

Also remember that the person who takes on the liquid during miles 0 to 20 will not falter in miles 20 to 26. The sporadic drinker will falter. Take your choice.

Principle 16. Enjoy the race. Remember, this is your day. You have worked hard and prepared well. The guidelines set forth in this book will help you finish this race. The race is a real high point. You deserve the success. Savor the victory. As the race wears on and things seem to be falling apart, slow your pace a little bit. The overall goal is to finish. If you've prepared well, you will.

The Second Time Around

Now you have a marathon under your belt. You've experienced the joys and frustrations, the agony and the ecstasy. Now you have some idea of what happens in a race. You know you can improve your time. Instinctively, you know where your weaknesses are.

To run a second race simply follow the preceding 16 principles. And add these few more.

Principle 17. Do more speed work. If you want to knock 15 minutes off your previous time, for example, speed work can help you. Set aside one day a week to go at a faster pace than you intend to run the marathon. Let's say your new goal is a 3:15 marathon. That's about a 7:30 pace. You might try running five miles at a 7 minute pace once a week. Or you might speed up slightly in one segment of your regular training runs. Let's say that you run 60 minutes a day. Six to 10 minutes might be at a faster pace.

Principle 18. Get involved in more and more races. There's nothing like racing to quicken your pace. Pick races that are 5,000 to 20,000 kilometers in length. An occasional 30 km is okay. Run these every two or three weeks. They are much like a marathon, only a lot shorter. Here you can go a lot faster. Just remember, for every two kilometers you race, take at least one day off for recovery. That means easy training.

Principle 19. Increase your mileage. The marathon is a mileage based race. If you have a good mileage base, your times are bound to come down. Dr. Paul Slovic did a study several years ago that showed that the success of marathon runners was contingent upon a runner's training mileage two months before the run. For example, he found that the sub-three hour runners averaged nine miles a day or 63 miles a week. The 3:01 to 3:30 marathoners ran six miles a day or 42 miles a week. The 3:31 to 4:00 runners averaged five miles a day or 35 miles a week. And the 4:01 and up marathoners averaged four miles a day or 28 miles a week. The verdict: go long.

Principle 20. Go on extra long training runs. Our training schedule in this book calls for weekly runs of about two hours at most, once a week. Research suggests that a 2½ to 3 hour run occasionally— maybe three times or so in the three months prior to the run—may be advantageous. These runs may be 20 miles or more. That recommendation may sound contradictory. Earlier we said you were to keep your runs under 20 miles. But here we are no longer talking to a beginning marathoner. You already have one under your belt. So the extra long runs may be helpful to you.

Principle 21. Lose some weight. In a marathon, your weight will significantly affect your performance. We have heard of runners who have said that they always wanted to weigh 200 pounds and look like O. J. Simpson. But when running the marathon they wished they weighed only 125. Extra weight slows you down.

Of course, our recommendation that you lose weight and fat is based on the assumption that you have a few pounds of fat to shed. Generally, the lighter you are, the fewer the orthopedic problems. Think about it: your feet hit the ground 1,000 to 1,200 times per mile. Would you rather have 125 pounds hitting the pavement or 180? Secondly, the lighter you are, the more efficiently you move. For every 1 percent drop in weight there is a corresponding 1 percent gain in oxygen consumption. That's significant. The amount of oxygen you are able to consume is one of the most important determinants of how well you'll do in running.

Principle 22. Do some hill training. Hill training will strengthen your hip flexors, quadriceps, and calf muscles. The hills will also improve your aerobic capacity or oxygen consumption. Hills will also give you confidence in training and improve your performance during marathon running.

Competition

After you have two marathons under your belt, you will probably be doing some serious thinking about how you can improve your times even more. Again, review the principles outlined (except for #1). But you can do more. There are additional principles you can use to improve your times. These principles are based on concepts advocated by Ron Daws in his book, *The Self-Made Olympian*. Daws, as his book title implies, was an Olympic marathoner in 1968.

Principle 1. Develop aerobic capacity and general endurance. Once you are able to do one long run (20 miles minimum for experienced runners) and two or three moderately long runs (10 to 15 miles) your goal is not to go farther but faster. These fast runs, however, are to approach, but not exceed, maximum ability. According to Daws, "For training purposes, one's maximum aerobic capacity at any point can be approximated by guessing the mile pace at which one could run a marathon."

Also during the week include one workout that covers hilly forest paths. That should be interspersed with fast and slow running. You might begin with a couple of easy miles and then repeat sections of a 5:00 to 6:30 pace or until pleasantly tired.

That training is extremely important. But you cannot participate in this kind of effort unless you have built an adequate base, followed our marathon training program, adequately adhered to all the principles, and completed two marathons.

Principle 2. Develop your power and stamina. According to Daws, this is best done by increasing the resistance. He advocates hill running, running in sand, in water, up stairs, and into the wind.

Quarter-mile and/or half-mile hills are probably best. If you happen to live in Indiana, Michigan, or Illinois and find few hills it may be necessary to run the interstate highway embankments. (These can be a bear.) If none are available you may do some wind running. That is, run into a stiff breeze.

When you do hill training, you should do it about three times a week. Be certain you keep the long run, but you might cut your week's mileage by about 10 to 20 percent.

Principle 3. Learn to maximize your capacity to

Running up stairs will develop your power and stamina.

Emil Zatopek ran in place for two hours in a tub of laundry rather than miss a workout.

tolerate anaerobic work and pace. You'll also want to increase your efficiency at faster speeds. According to Daws, "Tolerance to anaerobic work is developed by performing difficult anaerobic work, so interval training now becomes of value. It can be performed on the track, but it is usually best to use the track only to check progress."

When you begin this interval work it is best that you start slowly. Do not, we repeat, do not start with fast runs or sprints. Over the weeks, slowly pick up your pace. When your fitness level improves, then you can go faster and faster. In the beginning, you might do slow running with short rests and then gradually move into faster runs with more rest. Finally, you can do fast workouts and rest a little between runs.

We don't think more than two or three days a week of interval work is needed. Quite frankly, it's better to do less interval work than too much. Interval work can drive you up the wall.

Principle 4. Be flexible. By being flexible we mean flexible. For example, use any wasted time for training. If you have 30 minutes each day of wasted time, use it for training. That can be somewhere between 21 to 28 miles extra a week. That 21 to 28 miles can mean the difference between a 3:01 marathon and a 2:55 marathon or better.

You'll probably be able to come up with 101 excuses why you can't run on a particular day. But that's all they are, excuses. Some people have been very innovative in terms of their training. Emil Zatopek, who won the 5,000, 10,000 meters, and the marathon in the 1952 Olympic Games, would run in place for two hours in a tub of dirty laundry rather than miss a workout. Now that's dedication. Other runners that we have known have ridden bicycles, cross-country skied, even swam when injured or when conditions prevented them from running. Others have run on stairs or treadmills. They really want to drop their times and be highly competitive. If you share that desire, develop the attitude that nothing can stop you.

Principle 5. Don't worry about setbacks or mis-

Cross country skiing is an effective training method if conditions prevent running.

takes. You may get injured, develop a cold, or have some problem which curtails your activity. It will drive you up the wall but it's best to rest, recover, and then go back full bore. If you try to go back too soon, you'll be headed for trouble. Try your best to rest and to give your body a chance to recover.

Principle 6. If your training schedule works for you, stick to it. Don't jump from pillar to post. If something doesn't seem right then it may be time to change. But if you continue to make improvement you must be doing something right.

The worst thing you can do is to change your training right in mid-stream when you are having success. You should have confidence in your abilities and in your training regimen. You should know what is best for you. Don't worry about what you read or hear from other people. You know what's best for you.

Of course, this doesn't mean you should have a closed mind. You may want to beg, borrow, and steal from other people. It's just that once you have a philosophy, stick to it.

Charles T. Kuntzleman is a fitness consultant who put together Rating the Exercises and The Complete Book of Walking for CONSUMER GUIDE® magazine.

Running With The Pack

Detroit Free Press Marathon—1978
by Lyn Cryderman

5:00 am

I awoke after a restless night of half-sleep. Natural-ly, each dream previewed the race that I would run later that morning. My worst fear—waking at ten and missing the start—did not materialize. I was wide awake.

5:45 am

I began my ritualistic dressing procedure. Vaseline petroleum jelly between the toes. Vaseline between my legs. Vaseline under my arms. Band-Aid plastic strips over my nipples. No jock, but two pairs of cotton underwear. An old, well worn pair of cotton shorts. A new, cotton T-shirt. I had heard this was not wise, but I thought I'd gamble. Especially since it was given to me by the owner of Wiard's Orchards. He thought it would be great advertising. While it wasn't exactly a free pair of Adidas shoes with a hundred dollar bill in each one, it boosted my ego. At this point, my ego needed a boost.

5:50 am

As I was pulling on a thin pair of tube socks, my wife brought me a steaming cup of ginseng tea. My original plan did not include any exotic ergogenic aids, but at the pre-race party the night before, a very unhealthy looking salesman was giving out free samples, explaining that it aided endurance and that he could supply me with a more substantial supply at a ridiculous price. In the final moments before running 26 miles 385 yards, it's amazing how vulnerable you become to such gimmicks. I took the sample.

5:55 am

It was almost time to go. I laced on my shoes. They

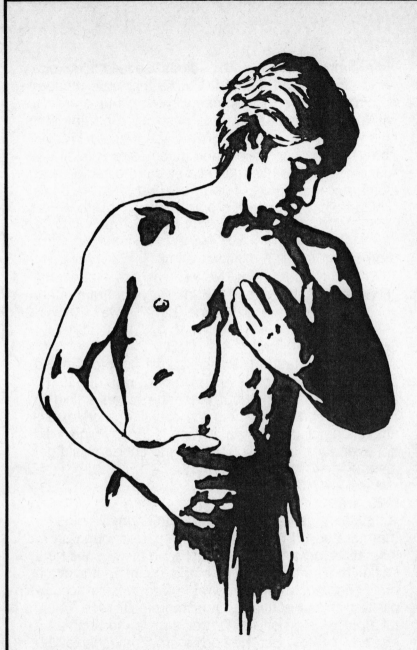

Before a race, apply petroleum jelly to your body.

were simple, unassuming. Adidas Gazells, blue with white stripes. I am unable to wear the more modern running shoes with flared heels and built-up arches. I wish I could because they look so neat, but my feet hurt when I wear them. FREE ADVICE #1: Forget about fashion and style when it comes to choosing a running shoe. Not everyone can wear the same shoe. Comfort is imperative. If your feet hurt after five miles during training, they will drop off after 26 miles, if you make it that far.

6:00 am

We left. No ceremony. No well-wishers. Not even a "good luck" from anyone. I had always heard runners do not run for fame or fortune, but this was absurd.

6:10 am

Denny's restaurant. Pancakes, of course. And, a cup of hot, black coffee. This, in part, was due to my addiction to caffeine, but also due to an article in *Runner's World* endorsing the practice prior to running a long distance. I was willing to try anything. I did not even consider how ginseng and coffee would get along.

6:20 am

I made a trip to the restroom. During my training for the marathon, I had been unfortunate enough on at least three occasions to be forced to the bushes for a bowel movement. I train in the country, and such practices, though uncomfortable, are at least accomplished in semi-privacy. This morning's race would take place along one of Detroit's main thoroughfares and I could not trust my body's timing mechanism to coincide with the "johns" that would be spaced approximately five miles apart. This is at least worth considering for future marathoners.

6:30 am
We left Denny's and headed into the blackness for Belle Isle. The race would not start until 9:00 am, but I was anxious.

7:00 am
The brochure said to meet at the Belle Isle Casino to catch a shuttle bus to the starting line, but I really hadn't expected the scene that greeted me. Up to this point, the city had been deserted. Now, however, I emerged onto a small island that was bustling with activity. Parking spots were scarce, even at this early hour. Buses came and went, while people of all shapes and sizes in jogging suits milled about. And it was still dark. I found a spot to park, checked one last time to see if I had left anything behind, locked the car, and walked with my wife toward the buses.

7:10 am
I must admit at this point I felt terrible. Perhaps it was the realization that once I entered the bus, there was no turning back. Perhaps seeing the multitude of runners made me realize that this was really something big and that a novice like me had no reason being there. Maybe it was the ginseng/coffee mixture. In any event, when I kissed my wife and stepped up into the neon lit coach, I felt like a prisoner being carted off to the torture chamber. It was all I could do to keep from crying.

7:40 am
The bus ride seemed to calm me down a bit, but the

real treat was what awaited me at the starting area. The sun was rising over the Detroit skyline, a large freighter was gliding noiselessly upriver, fish were finning the glassy-smooth surface of the water, and suddenly I realized again how wonderful it was to be alive, healthy, and able to even consider running 26 miles. Sure there was a risk. Sure I might not make it. Nothing of any worth is obtained without expense. As I jogged along the water's edge, breathing deeply the cool, morning air, the fear and tension were replaced with a calm assurance that whatever the outcome, I was prepared to face the test. If I finished, so be it. If I failed, so be it.

7:55 am
There were two thousand runners starting this race and it was a stirring sight to see them gathering in the starting area. Practically every age and body type were there. I had learned a few months earlier at a road race that you do not necessarily judge a runner by his size or stride. In that race I had been passed by the fleet of foot and the flat of foot. The short fat ones beat me as well as the tall thin ones. Though 29 and approaching the distance runner's prime age, I was overtaken by runners fifteen years younger and thirty years older. Here in the starting area were runners as young as 7 and older than 70. Now I knew better than to try and predict. As far as I was concerned, they were all great just for being there. I soon discovered that they thought the same of me. One of the uncanny things about distance running is that everyone is friendly. There seems to be no "psyching" like that associated with most other sports. Advice is passed around freely. Smiles abound. It's a festive atmosphere. And it's contagious.

8:15 am

My serious warm-up began. I had been jogging and walking since arriving, but I didn't feel that was enough. In recent weeks, I had been plagued by a minor strain in my groin. If I didn't finish, I reasoned, it would be due to this injury.

8:30 am

Everything felt good. When I jogged, the groin problem was there, but not very noticeable. I debated whether to lace my shoes tightly or loosely. I compromised. In the pocket of my sweat shirt I found a headband. It was a present from my wife. I had never worn one in training, but she felt I should wear it to keep the sweat out of my eyes. I wear contacts. I put on the headband and jogged some more.

8:40 am

We started to gather near the starting line. Believe it or not, out of two thousand runners I bumped into a couple of friends. We were all glad to see one another and gathered for some fellowship and a time of quiet prayer. We expressed gratitude to Him for health and asked nothing more of Him than safety and wisdom.

8:50 am

What a trip! A helicopter was buzzing us while a photographer leaned out the window snapping pic-tures. There was a mobile television crew, reporters, a bagpipe band, and well-wishers. Race organizers held signs designating pace. All the five minute per mile group were at the front. 5:30, 6:00 minutes, finally they got back to the eight minute per mile and beyond. I jumped in at the 8:30 section, not really sure yet of what I wanted to do. My only goal was to finish and I had been training at about seven minutes a mile. I knew that was too fast for the marathon, but didn't want to get too far back.

8:59 am

I thought: "Well, this is it!" Everyone pushed close, which was really stupid and we all knew it. "Just shoot the gun. We want to RUN!"

9:00 am

BANG! There was a cheer, but no one ran yet, At least not back where we were. We couldn't! In fact, we walked for at least the first minute. Soon, there was enough room to jog very slowly. I hit my pace after a couple of minutes. I wasn't really prepared for the surge of adrenalin brought on by the cheers of the crowd lining the street. It took all the self-discipline I could muster to hold my pace. I felt like sprinting. I felt like yelling. Many runners were. It was crazy! It was fun! I could think of no better place to be at nine o'clock on a Sunday morning.

9:30 am

We entered the Windsor-to-Detroit Tunnel. I felt a bit tired at this point, which alarmed me because we had only gone about three miles. I began to wonder about the heat. It was close to seventy at the start. Halfway through the tunnel we began a seven degree climb that would last for a half mile. I was running with a group that included a 77-year-old man. It was his first marathon too. He was working hard—too hard, I thought. I wished him luck and soon lost track of him.

9:38 am

We emerged from the tunnel to a throng of cheering

people. I saw signs that said, "We're proud of you, Dad!" People reached out to touch us. They were smiling. They envied us. They really wanted us to finish. I had a lump in my throat and felt like laughing and crying at the same time. Was I crazy?

At this point, time is forgotten. Though I wore a watch, I do not recall ever looking at it. I will now refer to miles.

5 Miles

We ran through Greektown and approached the first of the aid stations. I didn't really feel like drinking anything, but took a glass of water anyway. I knew that I might lose track of my fluid intake later on in the race and figured the best way to be consistent would be to take a little at each official aid station (every 2½ miles), but accept nothing in between. I sipped a little, then poured the rest over my face. It felt good, and snapped me out of a low point.

7½ Miles

I felt great! I thought: "If this keeps up, it will be a piece of cake." I really had to restrain myself. There was absolutely no pain in my groin. My wind was good. My legs and feet felt fine. Even the warm sun didn't seem to bother me. I was just a bit off eight minutes per mile.

10 Miles

Still no problems. I felt fortunate. Already I had seen several stop. The majority had shoe or foot problems. One was running with one shoe on while carrying the other in his hand. His bare foot was bleeding. We all urged him to stop. His face was blank. He ran on. I passed him, but didn't feel very good about it. At the aid station I sipped some water. Some stopped to walk while they drank. I didn't. As I tipped my head back to drink I choked and coughed. It was close. "Next time," I thought, "I'll stop." On I went.

12½ Miles

For some reason, I considered this the halfway point, even though it wasn't. I was still running smoothly and felt quite strong. My stomach was bothering me a little, but it was nothing that really worried me. We were running through a very wealthy section of the city and the homes were beautiful. Throughout the race you could not go a block without passing spectators. They were really helpful. They shouted encouragement. Many offered water, juice, candy, or gum. Without them I'm sure I would have been fighting a mental battle to keep going. It was at this point that I really had to concentrate. Physically, I felt okay. Not fine, but okay. Mentally, I was beginning to question, to doubt. What will happen when I hit the "wall"? How much will it hurt? What will go first, my legs or my wind? Having people along the way shaking your hand, patting you on the back, telling you you look great (lies, but I loved it) was a tremendous help.

13 Miles

This was not an official station, but someone held up a sign saying "You are halfway there!" Minor problems, again, of the mental nature, began. I experienced a little confusion. I thought the 12½ Mile mark was about two miles back. We turned into the wind. Wind has always bothered me. A little girl was handing out orange and yellow candy corns. I abandoned my race plan and took one, thinking the sugar would be good for some quick energy. Immediately, I choked. I couldn't get it all down. Worse yet, it made me terribly thirsty. I kept looking for the next aid station. I needed some water. I also needed to know where I was.

15 Miles

At this point I was utterly jubilant. I was convinced I would make it. No doubts. My legs were strong. I was breathing fine. I couldn't believe there was no pain in my groin. I had no blisters. I gave in and picked up the pace a bit. There were more people here and I was passing runners. I thought: "Just a quick ten miles to the finish"—a mistake I would pay for dearly. FREE ADVICE #2: Patience is a virtue in marathon running. No matter how great you feel along the way, stick to your original plan. After running fifteen miles or so, you do not think rationally. At this point, do not listen to your body, for it will deceive you.

17½ Miles

Still felt good. I couldn't believe it in fact. In training I had never run farther than thirteen miles at one time. But, here I was after more than 17 miles, feeling I could run forever. I tried to figure what the deal was. Suddenly, I realized the folly of the last 2½ miles. I eased up the pace, but soon found out it was too late.

18½ Miles

I was working a little harder now. But I still had no doubts about finishing. My legs were heavy. But my wind was good. My left foot was a little hot. I reviewed my pre-race plans: "Don't compensate by running on the side of my foot." I wondered out loud: "Where's that 20 Mile mark?" Here I was no longer passing, but being passed. Occasionally a woman went by. Was I embarrassed? I don't think so. I shouted encouragement and meant it. Reverse sexism? I don't know.

I was searching for the 20 Mile mark. A girl on a bike must have read my thoughts. "Six miles to go at the corner," she volunteered. I thought so. I assessed my situation: "Doing good. Legs heavy. Hot. Thirsty." I reached the corner. Funny, there was no aid station. The fate of stragglers? Even the empty cups were gone. Naturally, they had cleaned them up already. Just six miles to go. I thought, "I've just got to hang on."

20 Miles

Somewhere between the 17½ Mile mark and the 20 Mile mark I hit the wall. It was abrupt. One mile I felt good: the next mile I felt horrible. Everything went at once. The legs got heavy, my wind seemed spent, my spirit was struggling. My thighs actually ached. I was terribly thirsty but my stomach was uneasy. I think the time was somewhere around three hours. I couldn't remember. I passed a group of onlookers. I heard a male voice. It said, "These are the ones that probably won't make it." For the first time I seriously doubted my chances of finishing.

21 Miles

I crossed the bridge to Belle Isle. My wife met me halfway and ran with me. I was glad to see her but probably didn't show it. I experienced the orneriness I had read about. I was angry. I didn't want to talk. I had trouble negotiating a curb and inwardly cursed the race promoters for putting curbs on Detroit's streets. Someone told me there were about five miles to go. That made me mad. I wanted only two or three. I felt that was all I could take. Yet I knew they were probably right. My thighs screamed for relief. I needed more oxygen. Where was the aid station? I was now grabbing anything anyone would hand me to drink. Many were walking. It was hell.

23 Miles

I was on the back side of the island. I knew it was straight north until I reached a turn. Once I made the turn it would be almost over. Where was that turn? To my left was the finish line, not 300 yards away. I could hear the rousing music of the University of Michigan marching band. I could see runners finishing. It angered me further that I wasn't also enjoying the relief the finish must bring. Would I ever know it? Before, I had felt I could crawl the last three miles if I had to. Now, I was sure I couldn't. Each step hurt. Should I walk? Many were. I had heard once you stop you can't get going again. Who cared? I tried to walk. I couldn't. Two big knots developed in my thighs and I knew if I kept walking I would fall to the ground, gripped by muscle cramps. It was the ultimate cruelty. I was too tired to run, yet I couldn't walk.

24 Miles

I didn't want to hold on. Still no sign of the turn. My wife met me again. I told her I couldn't go on. I apologized for spending so much time away from the family, training for failure. I told her I hurt. She said she was proud and that she would see me at the finish. I kept running.

25 Miles

Finally, I hit the turn. Just around the bend and I should see the banner of the finish line. But wait.

Another turn. Not north again! It couldn't be. To the left was the finish. But I was to turn right. How far? Someone says two miles. I wanted to quit. In fact, at this point I came the closest to quitting. I had never known such pain. I was running on instinct. There was no will, no desire. I wanted to die.

25½ Miles

I was running south now. No more turns. Everyone along the roadside was shouting. No one was specific, but the finish was just "a little bit further ahead." It was going to happen. I think I was smiling. There it was. Only six hundred yards. I heard the band. I tried to go faster. I couldn't. Someone was running toward me. It was my wife. I told her I could make it. I tried to shout, but I couldn't. I wanted to sprint, but I couldn't. The road veered slightly to the right. I stumbled trying to follow it. I felt like crying. I felt like laughing. I could hardly breathe.

26 Miles, 385 Yards

The band was playing. People were cheering. An arm reached out and hugged me. It belonged to an attractive girl. She said, "You did it. You just ran the marathon." I had never seen her before. "I love you," I said. She laughed. "Well I love you too." She asked me if I was going to be alright. I said sure. Then she went back to her job of assisting the finishers. My time was 3:51. I spotted some orange juice. I drank about a quart. It was heavenly. My legs still wanted to run. I collapsed instead and lay in the beautiful sun.

Lyn Cryderman is an instructor of Teacher Education at Spring Arbor College (Michigan).

Running With The Best

Boston Marathon—1979
by Jeff Wells

6:30 am

I awoke after a pretty good sleep of 7½ hours. My roommate, John Lodwick and I dressed quickly and went to get some breakfast. We both ate very lightly—an English muffin, a piece of toast, and some orange juice. We then went back to the room to spend time with God in Bible study and prayer.

9:00 am

Ready, we left the room and drove to the starting point at Hopkinton. On the way over we talked about different things. I thought, "This is my 7th marathon. I hope I can do my best."

10:00 am

We reported to the high school gym to get our numbers. The school was jammed with people. Excitement was in the air. In the locker room I saw old friends. Don Kardong (4th in the '76 Olympic Marathon) and Benji Durden (11th in '78 at Boston and 2nd in '78 at Honolulu) in particular. It was good to see them again. I didn't feel too nervous but I could feel the electricity. I could feel the adrenalin building.

11:15 am

I did some warming up—about 35 to 40 minutes—at the high school. I did some stretching. A little loosening-up to get to the point where I could jog. Than I ran a half a mile or so—real easy. I did more stretching for 15 to 20 minutes and talked to Rick Rojas (a participant in the '75 Pan American Games Marathon) and another friend from Colorado Track.

11:40 am

I put on my shoes, used the restroom, and ran a

half mile down Hayden Rowe Street to the starting line on Route 135. At this point, I did four or five strides of 100 yards, commenserate with my marathon running pace. I felt pretty good. Ready. I ran out to the leaders in the front row. Their group was already packed. I squeezed in past the leaders and took a place in the second row. I recognized Randy Thomas (5th in '78 in Boston) and we talked a bit. I talked to a few other runners. Soon I heard my name called by Will Cloney—the Boston Athletic Club and Boston Marathon Race Director. He wanted me on the front row because of my previous best time— 2:13:15. I preferred to stay in the center of the second row.

We were crowded. Packed. My main thought was: "I don't want to fall. I've just got to stay afoot. If nothing else happens— just stay up, Wells." I put my elbows out a little bit to give me balance and some running room. The weather was good. The temperature was in the high 40's with a slight headwind. Not much humidity. Good weather for a marathon.

12:00 noon

Bang. The gun was fired and we were off. I think: "Whew, I'm off in one piece. No one else falls—good. That can happen so easily in such a crowded start. Thanks, Lord. This feels good. Exciting. The old adrenalin is pumping." The first 100 or 200 yards are exciting at Boston. I'm not among the front runners. I'm about 20 to 30 yards back of #1.

After a few hundred yards I see Bill Rodgers. He sees me and says hi. Then he runs past me. He's running at a quicker pace than I am. I feel pretty good though. I'm running well—not killing myself—but staying pretty close to the leaders.

The first mile of Boston seems to be pretty much downhill. The next two to three miles roll slightly but there is a slight downward grade. Sometimes you make the mistake of running too fast at this point in the race. The course leads you through the town of Ashland.

Three Miles
By this point the running packs had formed. The first was established and consisted of Bill Rodgers (1975 Boston winner, American record holder), Frank Shorter (1972 Olympic champion, 1976 silver medalist), Esa Tikkanen (3rd in '78 in Boston), Tom Fleming (2nd in'75 in Boston), and four or eight other guys. Our pack (the second one) was not as well formed. But it was building. Randy Thomas, Rick Rojas, Jack Fultz (1976 Boston winner), Yutaka Taketomi (9th in '78 in Boston), Don Kardong, and myself.

Jerome Drayton (1977 Boston winner) was also in the front pack. I was about 30 yards behind Drayton. It was here, however, that I saw Drayton peel off to the side and throw his gloves down. Disgusted, he quit running—a hamstring injury.

Four to Six Miles
The groups were well formed by four miles. I was in the second group and running pretty strong. I thought I'd run with this group most of the race. I like running with a group. If someone gets a drink in a group he might offer it to others in the pack. I was also conscious of the headwind here. It wasn't bad, but I knew it was there.

At five miles we came to the big clock. I couldn't tell if the minute hand was at twenty-four or twenty-five. I think it was under 25. The pace had seemed fast. We were clipping miles off at a pace faster than five minutes a mile. That pace felt good. The lead group with Rodgers was about 50 to 70 yards ahead of us. They seemed to be going too fast for me at this point. I didn't have any desire to be up there. I didn't want to make a move to go up at this time. It was a long race. Plenty of time to move up.

Six to Seven Miles

At about the six mile point there had been a course change this year. I didn't recognize it until we were coming out of it. The course was smooth. I liked the change. At the 7 Mile mark we came up to our first water station. John Lodwick, Kevin McCarey, and I had made arrangements with Geoff Hollister, our shoe representative with Nike, to have squeeze bottles of ERG, the athletic drink. Other aid stations we had planned were for 12, 17, and 20 miles. The liquid felt good at this point and all went well. Although I wasn't too thirsty here I knew I would need it later on. The lead group seemed to be gaining on us. They were about 100 to 150 yards ahead.

Seven to Twelve Miles—Framingham, Natick, and on to Wellesley

The crowd was encouraging. The people were getting thicker all the time. Especially when going through the towns. Most of the time I ran with Randy Thomas. The people were yelling: "Let's go Randy." (Randy lives in Boston.) I felt good at this point. I was conscious of the small hills, however. Boston seems to be continuously hilly—both up and down. The hills were no big deal here. But I knew they were there.

During this five or six mile stretch I started to think about my hard training the past week. Seven days before, I did a hard run of 10 miles at about (or near) a five minute pace. The next day I did interval 880's. The third day I ran about (or near) race pace for 7½ miles and on the 4th day I ran about (or near) race pace for 5 miles. The last three days of the week I went light. I had never done that kind of hard training that close to a race. I was concerned. But I relied on God to take care of my recovery.

I started assessing my body here. I wanted to be aware of where I was hurting. I wanted to know how I was doing. Everything checked out okay. My calves seemed to lack springiness. They weren't tight, but they didn't seem to be as strong as I'd like.

The crowd was a great inspiration here. They took my mind off being tired, somewhat. I started thinking about John Lodwick (my roommate and 8th in '78 in Boston). I wondered where he was. I knew he was behind me somewhere. But where, I didn't know. At the start he was ahead of me. But I passed him about a mile out. I hadn't seen him since. I said a short prayer for John to have strength.

At this point Randy Thomas started pulling ahead. The crowds were really pulling for him. I figured he felt he should try to catch the lead pack.

Thirteen to Sixteen Miles—Wellesley to Charles
I'm still running with Don Kardong, Rick Rojas, Yutaka Taketomi, and Jack Fultz. It was here we started gradually moving up on the lead pack. I was running very closely with Don Kardong. Jack Fultz and Yutaka Taketomi were back a bit. Rick Rojas dropped back even more and soon dropped out of the race.

Randy was now well ahead of us. About midway between the lead pack and us. It was here that the race seemed toughest to me mentally. I didn't feel real bad at this time but I didn't feel real good either. In a marathon you have highs and lows. This was one of those lows. I just didn't seem to be strong.

Between 15 and 16 miles, Kardong and I pulled slightly ahead of the second pack. Shorter had dropped off the lead pack and we passed him. I felt sorry for him. People were yelling, "Come on, Frank." But he was obviously tired. Gosh, I thought, it must be tough on him. As I passed him I wanted to say something. Not too much, just some words of encouragement, So I said, "Let's go, Frank." But that was the last I saw him.

Sixteen to Twenty-One Miles

The hills start here. I was still running with Kardong. He gained a few yards on me going up the hills. I was forced to watch him forge ahead. But going down was another story. My coach, Harry Johnson, had shown me a new downhill running technique. "Right before your foot hits the ground, you rotate your foot forward so you don't land on your heels. The weight falls more on the front of your foot, not on the ball, but more towards the front." It worked, for I'd catch Kardong going down. But he'd catch me going back up. With every downhill, however, I would repeat Harry Johnson's advice.

There are five hills. And while they are not particularly tough they are difficult because they come in a hard part of the race. In 1977, I was in second place going into the last hill. I even passed Rodgers here. But the hills took it out of me. They killed me. I had to walk and jog the last mile in 1977 because of fatigue. I was passed by 10 other runners in the last 6 miles. I finished 12th.

This year I hoped to avoid the same mistake. So I ran the hills conservatively. Maybe too conservatively. But I didn't want to push too hard and leave it all there. Kardong and I jostled along these hills for two miles. But finally I pulled ahead of him. And he never came back to me. I was in 5th place and running well.

All of a sudden on the last hill Jack Fultz pulled past me. I was quite surprised. I'm really stronger in the last part of the race and here's Fultz passing me. I felt good. But Fultz must have felt better. He passed me as many lead runners do—very quickly. (They don't want to move too gradually on anyone and then have them run with them—it makes it easier to run.) But after getting 10 yards ahead of me, I noticed Fultz didn't pull away.

The crowds were really getting thick. Four to six deep. They were yelling our names. I felt good. Many were offering me a drink. It was exciting and my adrenalin was high. The crowd and the adrenalin helped keep my mind off my tiredness. I felt a lot better than last year. That made me feel even better. We reached the top of Heartbreak Hill (the last one). I was relieved. What a load off my back. I was through the hills and still felt good.

Twenty-One Miles

At the top of the hill I thought I should really push. I felt too good for only having four or five miles to go in the race. When the race was over I didn't want to have anything left. I wanted total effort. It would be tragic to finish and have something left.

We started downhill. Things were really getting crowded. In fact it seemed as though the path was only two or three yards wide in some spots. Going downhill, I again used the downhill running technique.

I started gaining on Jack, and soon passed him. I was now again in 5th place. Rodgers was in 1st. Tikkanen was 2nd, Kevin Ryan was 3rd, and Randy Thomas 4th. They were about 100 to 150 yards ahead of me, maybe more.

Twenty-Two to Twenty-Four Miles

With four miles to go I thought I could probably catch Thomas, Ryan, and Tikkanen if I ran strong and steady. So I ran very hard. Probably harder than I ran in the entire race up until this point, except for the first few miles that were all downhill. I think I was well under 5 minutes a mile at this point. I steadily moved up on them. Because the gap was closing, my confidence was boosted. All four of the leaders were pretty well split apart by now. It was Rodgers in first; 100 to 150 yards back was Tikkanen; 30 yards in back of him was Ryan; and 50 yards behind Ryan was Randy Thomas.

I eased up to Randy and caught him. As I passed Randy I asked him how far we had to go. He didn't hear me at first or I didn't hear his answer. So I asked him again. I felt pretty good. But after running that far at this pace I was tired and didn't want to run forever. I was concerned that it not be too far. He told me we had 2½ miles to go. I was disappointed. I was hoping it wasn't that far. But I was still shooting for 2nd. I moved past Randy and steadily moved up. With a little more than two miles to go I passed Ryan. I continued to push the pace. I was running harder than I had the entire race. At two miles I caught Tikkanen. Here I could see Rodgers very well. The last several miles of the Boston Marathon are pretty much a straight run through the city. The crowd was now waving their arms and yelling, "Come on, you can catch him." I'm sure they were giving similar encouragement to Bill, shouting, "Let's go, you can win." Rodgers was about 100 yards ahead of me, maybe 120. I didn't really think too seriously that I could catch him. But the crowd on the route was waving me on. They kept encouraging me.

I was very tired and wanted to finish. But at the same time I had the feeling that the further the race would be, the better the chance I would have of catching Rodgers. I continued to move steadily toward him. The crowd was very thick on both sides. They closed in a little bit. I feared that maybe the crowd would push in and close us off. Then the race would be stopped. Or we'd have to fight our way through. Twice earlier in the race I had to squeeze in between the crowd and a vehicle or a press bus.

I continued to see Bill. And I seemed to be gaining on him. But it seemed as though he was just too far ahead. Impossible to catch. Yet there were fleeting moments when I thought I could catch him. [It was at this point that a policeman told Bill Rodgers that someone was gaining on him. Rodgers looked back and saw Wells coming and picked up his pace.]

Twenty-Five Miles to The Finish

With less than a mile to go I saw the Citgo sign. What a relief. The Citgo sign is where you turn to go up to the Prudential Building and the finish. It was reassuring. I was getting closer and closer to Bill as we moved toward the Prudential Building. With a half mile to go I thought I could catch him. But for a fleeting moment I thought maybe I shouldn't. "He's run in first place for so long. He's worked so hard. Maybe it's best not to catch him." But I rebuked myself for thinking that.

"That's not the right kind of attitude. I need to give 100 percent effort. God wants me to give 100 percent effort." I continued to run hard.

Bill rounded the corner onto Hereford Street which heads up to the Prudential Center. We had about 400 yards to go. I was about 30 yards behind him. I saw policemen on horses keeping the crowd back. The crowd was thick in the streets and they were hanging out of the windows and standing in doorways. The noise was deafening. Bill had to swerve to avoid one of the horses. It was here, with Bill almost up the hill and I halfway up the hill, that I decided to pull out all the stops. I wasn't going to save anything at this point. I was sprinting as hard as possible. I was trying to catch Bill. It didn't seem likely that I could catch him. But I had to go as hard as I could.

Bill was going hard. I was about 4 or 5 seconds behind him. Both of us were sprinting. I thought, "Maybe I can catch him." I vaguely remember seeing some guy run in front of me toward the end. Right between Bill and me. It didn't register, yet it did. It didn't interfere with me however.

The last 100 yards was all out. The area was jammed with people. I still thought I might be able to catch Bill. I was very tired. But the race was no longer mentally tough. The finish was near. We had about 40 yards to go. Bill was nearing the finish. I was gaining on him but I was not going to catch him.

The policeman who was following Bill stopped maybe 15 yards from the finish. Another policeman who was following him peeled off a bit and stopped. Both blocked my way. I was forced to jump a little. I had to go to the side. I was relieved that I didn't have an accident. I know it did not cost me the race because Rodgers had either finished or was about to finish. I was about 12 yards behind him.

In a matter of seconds I crossed the finish line. I was very tired. Very glad to finish. My dominant reaction was gratitude to God. It was a delightful surprise that I had finished 2nd. I wasn't disappointed—maybe just a little—but I had run my best time ever—2:10:15. Rodgers ran a 2:10:13.

[So ended the closest race in Boston Marathon History.]

Jeff Wells is a graduate student at Dallas Theological Seminary.

The Afterglow

by Charles T. Kuntzleman

The marathon is over. After months of preparation, hundreds or thousands of miles of running, and supreme dedication, you have reached your goal. Some first-time finishers say: "Never again." Others: "It's too much like childbirth—maybe later..." And still others: "Next time I'll do better."

We think that if you follow the principles outlined in this book you'll be ready for another. And you'll want to do better. Of course, fatigue will have already set in. But you'll want to do more running.

Right now, however, your body needs a break. That doesn't mean you have to stop running. You simply have to cut down on your mileage and intensity for a period of time. In other words, make your running easy and relaxed, laid back.

Recovery from a marathon begins as soon as you cross the finish line. At this point several things are apparent. Overall fatigue will be present. Maybe more fatigue than you've ever known. It may seem, however, that your legs don't want to stop moving. But you'll feel sore, strained muscles in your legs. You may also be experiencing blisters and skin burns— such as chafing in the groin. It is possible that you are breathless and you may be suffering from dehydration. Occasionally you may feel nausea and light-headedness. But the most frequent complaint is extreme, overall fatigue. Because of the fatigue and other problems previously mentioned, just stopping feels good. To help relieve or reduce this discomfort you might follow this advice.

First, walk around casually after finishing. After drinking some liquid and dressing, you might try walking another 15 minutes. This practice will help reduce some muscle soreness and stiffness.

Second, drink plenty of liquids, especially if the

weather is hot and humid. Do not rely on your thirst mechanism. Your body needs water. Your body has just not told you yet. Continue to drink plenty of liquids throughout the rest of the day. David Costill, Exercise Physiologist at Ball State University, Muncie, Indiana, has said, "During a marathon you can't even come close to replacing fluids you lose. Drinking at aid stations may replace only 1/10th of the fluid you lose. You are going to be markedly dehydrated. Immediately afterwards you should consume fluids to get rehydrated. You should incorporate some sugars in that drink so you could drink either fruit juices or some commercial athletic drinks that are available.

"The human thirst mechanism is quite slow. As a result you may be eight pounds dehydrated and have a couple glasses of fluid and feel satisfied. But an hour later, you will be thirsty again. It's a delayed reaction. Other animals are different. They rehydrate 100 percent at the first watering. But humans don't respond that way. You have to force yourself to drink some extra. Watch your body weight for the next 24 hours. Generally, this is enough time to get your fluids back."

Take Costill's advice. CHECK YOUR WEIGHT. Every two pounds of weight you have lost in the run is equivalent to about one quart of water. So, if you lose four pounds you need to replace two quarts of water, etc. The rehydration should take place during the first 24 hours after the race. The closer to the finish of the race the better.

Third, a hot/cold shower may be helpful. That is, start off with an ordinary hot shower then switch to cold water. Keep alternating. Hot and cold. Some runners simply prefer to lie down in a hot bath. Whether the better feeling of showers and baths is physiological or psychological is open to question. But most marathoners report better feelings after trying these techniques. Whether a shower or a bath is best will depend upon you.

Fourth, massage is helpful. There is no need to hire a masseur or masseuse. You can do it by yourself. Rub your muscles where they attach to the bone. The massage will help you relax the entire muscle.

Fifth, do the stretching exercises beginning on page 58. These exercises will help stretch muscles that are tightened after the long run. The repetiveness of the run causes the muscles at the back of the leg to be shortened significantly. The slow stretching helps to counteract the shortening.

Sixth, your diet after a marathon should be similar to what you ate before the marathon. Again Costill says "In order to recover as rapidly as possible, the obvious thing is to consume considerable carbohydrates." Probably the first meal after the marathon should be like the last big meal before. If you had spaghetti or some other heavy carbohydrate the night before, the meal after competition should be very much the same. You want to recover as much of that used up glycogen as possible.

It takes three to five days to recover the glycogen. That's part of the problem of recovering from a marathon. A lot of people don't go after the carbohydrates hard enough, and that is part of the cause for the fatigue and difficulty in getting back to running form again.

Some experts recommend taking on additional amounts of vitamin C and B complex. The research in this area is not clear. Generally, fresh fruits and vegetables will supply your essential needs. As in all good health practices, avoid junk foods as a means of getting calories.

All of this takes care of the first day. But what about 24 hours later? After all, the soreness seems to peak around 24 to 48 hours after the run.

Most medical authorities aren't sure what causes the soreness and stiffness. It's probably due to the waste products formed during the run and left in the fluid that surrounds the cells. That usually causes the pain during and immediately after the run. The pain that occurs 24 to 48 hours after the exercise is probably the result of muscle tears or localized contractions of muscles. Of course, the pain will gradually subside but it will be very real for several days. When walking up stairs your legs may feel as though they have been hit with a baseball bat.

Massage, stretching, walking, showers, hot soaks, light running will help relieve soreness even if only temporarily. And of these, the stretching will probably be best, though some runners report that light running and walking are also a great help. Ice massage on sore muscles will also aid in relieving soreness. Eight to ten minutes should be sufficient. You may also get relief by placing your legs higher than your head, periodically, during the day. This can be done right from the day of the marathon and for a week afterward.

The biggest question, of course, is when do you start running again? Surprisingly, you can start the next day. But unless you are a purist, it is probably best to take a couple of days off. Walk instead. Then begin easy running. You will probably find you won't feel as sharp for almost a month. That is, your legs won't seem to have the spring they had before the race. You may seem to tire more quickly on your runs.

The feeling is both physical and psychological. The physiological refers to the fact that your body hasn't recovered from the long run. The psychological refers to the fact that you may be a little bit depressed. Depression is a natural letdown after all those months of training.

Experts say that you should take one day to recover for each mile that you covered in the marathon. That is, 26 or 27 days. We recommend that you listen to your body. Run again when you feel that your body is ready to go. When you return to running, it is probably best to follow a program similar to that which you did prior to the stepped up three/six month marathon training plan. Run in a relaxed manner. Do this for about a month after the race. After that you're ready for stepped up training, if you wish.

Of course, during this month you'll want to take special care to adequately stretch before and after each training run.

If at any time you feel as if your injury may be more than muscular, that your bones hurt, for example, you may want to check with your doctor. Also, if you have blisters, you will want to make sure that these are properly taken care of.

The number of marathons you run each year is for you to decide. There are people who run 12 or more marathons a year. In fact, we know of people who have run marathons back to back. That is, one on a Saturday and another on a Sunday. For the beginner, running marathons is a significant enough goal, let alone running marathons back to back. The great majority of experts feel that there are only a few people whose bodies can handle this rigorous running. The great majority of runners should not run more than two marathons in a year's time.

You may run more than two, if you wish, but only two should be classified as hard. The other marathon runs should be considered training runs. More than that will affect adversely not only your performance but your health and general energy levels.

One more thing. It is so important that we have underscored it. *Enjoy your success.* You have obtained a significant milestone. You have run 26 miles, 385 yards. Congratulate yourself on a job well done. Remember, you are one out of just a few Americans who have run a marathon. You're unique. Over 220 million Americans have never run that far. That puts you into a special category. Enjoy! You deserve it.

After you complete a marathon, you can run into the sunset. You're a hero.

Charles T. Kuntzleman is a fitness consultant who put together Rating the Exercises *and* The Complete Book of Walking *for* CONSUMER GUIDE® *magazine.*

Consumer Guide® Magazine Evaluation Of Running Shoes

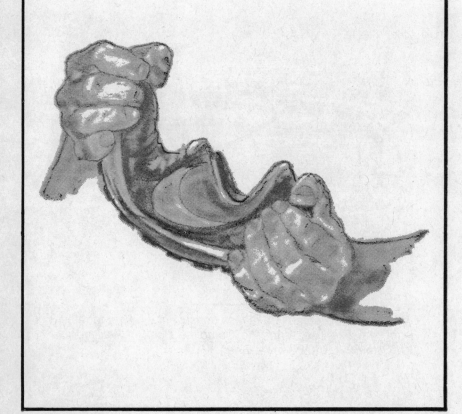

Without doubt, shoes are the most important equipment a runner owns. You can cover just as much territory in old shorts and a sweatshirt as you can in an expensive designer outfit, but a good pair of shoes means the difference between success and failure.

The feet of a runner take a lot of punishment and protecting them helps you to avoid injuries. In an ideal world, perhaps, we could all run barefoot through meadows. Reality is different. Most of us have worn shoes from early childhood and our feet are accustomed to them. In addition, we do most of our running on pavement, hard roads, or packed-down tracks—all much rougher on the feet than springy grass.

There are, as always, exceptions to this rule. Abebe Bikila, the famous Ethiopian marathoner, won an Olympic Gold Medal by running barefoot through the streets of Rome. This astounding performance should be admired but not copied. All authorities agree that shoes are the one item you should not skimp on. "Nothing, in fact," says Bob Anderson, founder and publisher of *Runner's World,* "is as important as a good pair of running shoes." He considers shoes so vital to successful running that his magazine devotes an entire issue each year to a comprehensive evaluation of the various brands on the market. So, buy the best pair of shoes you can afford. They are an excellent investment.

Where To Buy Shoes

Only a few years ago, it was difficult to find shoes designed specifically for running. Most people had to be content with tennis shoes, sneakers, or other "sport" shoes. Today the situation is different. There are many excellent models designed for running that are readily available. Ordinary sports stores, some department and shoe stores, and shops catering specifically to runners carry the kinds of shoes you want.

The problem with these stores is that you may not be able to find one that carries the one brand you really want. If you live outside a metropolitan area or some place where running is not yet popular, you are liable to become frustrated. The names and addresses of the major manufacturers are listed at the end of this chapter. Write or call them to find out what stores in your vicinity carry their products.

Another possibility is a mail-order dealer. Although you will not be able to inspect or try on the shoes before you purchase them, in almost all cases you can return the shoes if you are not happy with them. Be sure to send them pencil tracings of your feet along with the size. When you get the shoes, try them on as soon as they arrive, walk around the house in them, and run in place. If the fit is not right or there is some other feature that makes them impractical for your feet or your running, send them back immediately. Don't wear the shoes outside, however, or you will not be able to return them.

Selecting Your Shoes

Finding the right shoe can be a bit complicated. There are so many brands on the market that it is difficult to choose. Personal preference plays a big role. What works for one person may not work for another. It comes down to this: if the shoe you have works for you, stay with it. When problems occur, look for common-sense solutions.

The following are our suggestions about what to

consider when shopping for running shoes. To make sure you understand the terminology on the following pages, we have included a chart showing the structure of the shoe.

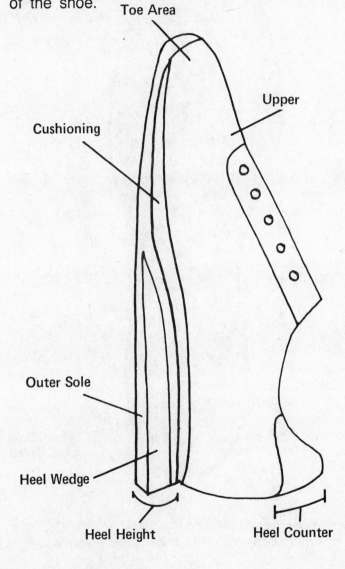

Toe Area

Upper

Cushioning

Outer Sole

Heel Wedge

Heel Height

Heel Counter

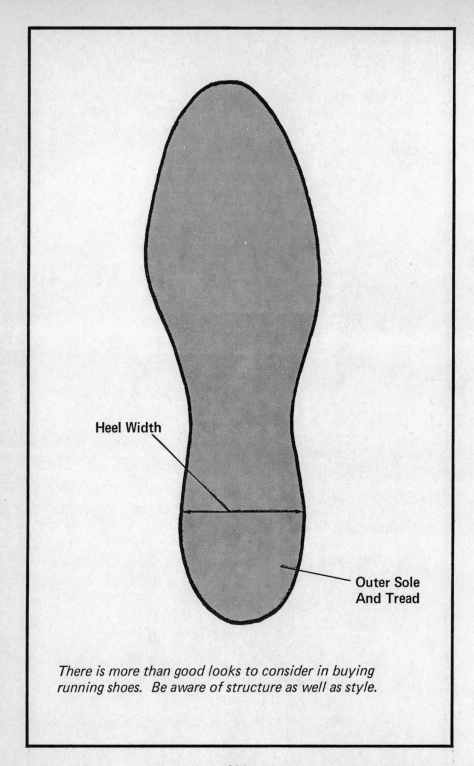

Heel Width

Outer Sole And Tread

There is more than good looks to consider in buying running shoes. Be aware of structure as well as style.

Fit. You, not the experts, will be wearing the shoes. So no matter how marvelous the design, if it isn't right for you, it's a waste of money. Your feet, like your fingerprints, are individual. You should make your selection with that in mind.

Begin by drawing an outline of your feet. Place each foot on a piece of paper and draw around it. (The lead of the pencil should follow the curvature of your instep.) Since one foot may be larger than the other, it's a good idea to trace both. When you go to the store, compare the bottom of each shoe to your tracing. How closely do the shoes conform to your feet? Are they wide enough across the ball and toe? Are they long enough?

When trying on shoes, wear the socks that you will use when running. If you plan to wear two pairs of socks, as many runners do, wear both.

Check the toe area with special care. When you run, your foot will slide forward inside the shoe. Allow about half an inch between your toe and the front of the shoe. Too snug a fit can cause undue pressure, blisters, black toes, and corns. Be sure that your toes have enough room to spread out a little bit.

Lacing. Currently there are three lacing patterns used in shoes. The most common is the U-throat or U-box, which is a full lacing pattern down to the toes in the shape of a U, much like the lacing pattern found on most dress shoes. The vamp, or bulcher, pattern runs across the instep of the foot and does not go all the way down to the toes. Recently, some shoe manufacturers have emphasized the speed-lacing arrangement. Here the laces pass through plastic or metal rings so the laces do not snag when they are being tied. Many U-box or bulcher patterns incorporate speed lacing.

Support. Because your foot hits the ground so many times during the course of a run, firm support is a must. Most shoes designed for running offer some measure of support, but they may not be sufficient for you. If the arch support in an otherwise excellent shoe seems inadequate, you can add foam rubber supports yourself. These inserts are readily available. Good built-in support is preferable, however.

Weight. Ordinary running shoes vary considerably (up to 25 percent) in weight. Weight can be a factor when running marathons.*

Flexibility. This is one of the more important factors in judging a shoe. Many injuries are caused by shoes that are too stiff. Unless the sole bends easily, your foot will suffer. Bend the shoe back and forth to test its pliability. The foresole must flex. If the sole at the ball of the foot is too stiff, then the Achilles tendon will be overstressed. The stress occurs because the leg works hard to bend the sole at the ball of the foot. If you weigh 200 pounds or more, you'll want more cushioning than sole flexibility. A shoe should not be flexible at the midsole or under the arch. If it is, the bottom of the foot will suffer from lack of support, and plantar fasciitis (a strain or partial rupture of the ligament that runs from the ball to the heel of the foot) will result.

Sole. All soles are made of rubber. They vary greatly in design. The sole must provide protection and cushioning while remaining flexible—no easy accomplishment. Most manufacturers solve the prob-

---

*A case could be made that for every extra ounce you carry it will result in a ton over 26 miles. You take 1200 steps a mile and 1200 times 10 ounces is 1200 ounces. That's the equivalent of 75 pounds a mile.

lem by providing double soles: a tough outer layer to resist impact; and one or more softer layers inside to cushion the feet and absorb shocks. This combination is definitely better than either hard or soft soles alone.

There also are distinctive tread designs. The trend today is toward the "waffle" tread, which is a series of raised grippers designed to provide greater traction. A number of patterns including square, round, star-shaped, and triangular grippers are offered by different companies. Because the shock of impact is borne by the grippers rather than by the whole foot, the waffle tread probably provides more cushioning than a flat tread. But pending further evidence, we believe that tread design is largely a matter of personal preference. (Pony Sports & Leisure, Inc. has a prototype shoe that uses air pumped into the sole through a small valve in the rear. The foot is supported on a cushion of air. The shoe is being developed by former Israeli Olympian Dr. Gideon Ariel. Nike has a model—Tailwind—that has inflated midsole channels.)

Heel. A moderately elevated heel is best. The shoe should place the heel of the foot higher than the front of the foot. Measure the forefoot thickness at the ball of the foot, and measure the shoe's heel height at the point of maximum thickness of the sole, where it meets the heel of the foot. *Runner's World* magazine says, "A shoe that has a forefoot sole thickness of 14mm should have roughly 26-29mm thickness in the heel area, or 12-16mm more in the heel than in the forefoot."

The shoe should hold the heel of the foot snugly without discomfort. Make sure that the top of the heel hits the back of your foot at a comfortable level. If it is too low, there will not be enough support; if it is extremely high, you may develop blisters or Achilles tendon problems. Compare the depth of the running shoe's heel with that of your regular shoes. The heel counter, the piece on the back of the shoe that supports the heel and Achilles tendon, should be firm and comfortable. The counter should be firm, and the heel tabs should be of adequate height to help stabilize the heel during contact with the ground. It should not be so high as to become a source of chafing. The heel width is measured at the widest point from one side of the ankle pad to the other.

Toe box. The toe box design is extremely important. When you're running downhill, your feet are forced forward in the shoes, so there should be at least a half inch of space between the tip of the longest toe and the inside surface of the front of the shoe. Most importantly, the toe box should be high enough to allow the toes to move freely. If the toe box is too low, the tops of the shoes will rub the tops of the toes and cause black toenails, blisters, and other toe problems. The toe box height is usually measured about one inch back from the inside top of the shoe.

Uppers. The uppers are the part of the shoe that gives it its distinctive appearance. Resist the temptation to judge a shoe by its color or sportiness. Function is more important. The upper must be firm enough to stabilize the foot and soft enough on the inside so that it doesn't irritate the foot. Avoid shoes with thick seams that may chafe.

Uppers are made of nylon, leather, or combinations of materials. Usually, nylon uppers are best because they are light, permit good air circulation, and are easy to clean. Leather is preferable if you plan to run a lot in inclement weather.

If you can afford it, buy two pairs of shoes. You

might prefer to have one pair for ordinary running and one pair for bad-weather running. The extra pair is really a luxury rather than a necessity, however.

It is important to purchase new shoes before the old ones are completely worn out. Wear the new ones on shorter runs to break them in. By the time you are ready to discard your old ones, the new ones will be comfortable.

Rating The Training Shoes

On the following pages, Charles T. Kuntzleman and the editors of CONSUMER GUIDE® magazine have listed four groups of excellent running shoes. These ratings employ Kuntzleman's opinions on the shoes, feedback he received on them from a great number of serious runners, and research conducted by leading authorities in the field of physiology.

Many of the factors mentioned as points to consider when buying running shoes cannot be judged easily by mere visual inspection, so the following ratings may be of help as you look at and try on several different brands. Naturally your own feet are going to be the best judge of how well a particular shoe works for you. But these ratings can give you an overall view of various designs, and their pros and cons. The following guide may save you time as you shop.

Highly Recommended Shoes For Men

Brooks Vantage. A special "varus wedge," as Brooks calls it, turns the feet slightly outward to compensate for the inward rotation of the foot when running. Central shock absorption is excellent because of the layered sole (two layers under the foot and three under the heel). Perhaps the best feature of the Vantage is its special inner sole that molds itself to the runner's foot, providing excellent front support. Nylon mesh uppers provide good air circulation. The only major disadvantage is that the sole is less durable than you expect on a quality product. The manufacturer says that the upper and sole of the 1978 version of the shoe are stronger and longer wearing than before. CONSUMER GUIDE® magazine rates this shoe an excellent buy.

Sizes: 4 to 13
Widths: Narrow, Medium, Wide

Brooks Vantage Supreme. This new shoe, introduced in 1978, is an excellent shoe. However, the Vantage by Brooks (above) is almost equal in quality and is $5 less. The shoe has U-box lacing and a special built-in support system insole.

Sizes: 4 to 13
Widths: One standard width

BROOKS VANTAGE

CONVERSE WC TRAINER 2

Converse WC Trainer 2. This top shoe is strong and durable, but it seems to be less comfortable than many of the other models. The shoe has suede reinforcement at the forefoot and heel areas and a high heel counter. It's a lighter shoe than their earlier model. The nylon mesh upper is unusually strong. Bulcher lacing is used. The heel counter is padded.
Sizes: 6 to 13
Widths: One standard width

New Balance 320. This is New Balance's most popular model. It comes in all the standard widths of regular shoes. This makes it easy to obtain the proper fit. The 320 also offers good shock absorption, particularly at the extra-wide heel. The one-piece polyester and suede upper has a padded tongue for greater comfort and flexibility. The padded heel counter provides excellent support. Sole durability, is questionable. The shoe has a flat tread. The toe box of the 1977 model was too narrow. This can cause black toenails, and blisters. But new space inside the toe box and a redesigned outer sole now provide greater roominess. This shoe is an especially good buy for runners with odd-sized feet.
Sizes: 3½ to 15
Widths: AA to EEEE

New Balance Trail 355. This brand-new shoe for 1978 has tested out very well. Made of polyester

NEW BALANCE 320

mesh with suede trim, the shoe is a good addition to the New Balance line. It has bulcher lacing with padded ankle and heel collars.
Sizes: 3½ to 15
Widths: AA to EEE

Nike LDV. The top Nike shoe has received great acclaim. It does not have great sole flexibility, but it has excellent sole wear and impact qualities. The extra-deep waffle tread and padded heel offer good cushion and protection. The solid rubber inserts at stress points in the heel are another asset. The uppers are of nylon mesh, with U-box lacing.
Sizes: 3 to 13
Widths: One standard width

Saucony Hornet. The Hornet's low price, light weight, and excellent heel construction make it a bargain. This year the manufacturer increased the

NEW BALANCE TRAIL 355

SAUCONY TRAINER 1980

midsole thickness, increased the wedge height, and gave it a lighter and more flexible sole. The heel is now more flared than it was last year. Construction of the shoe is excellent. The tread on the shoe is a herringbone pattern. The shoe has good flexibility and impact qualities. But its sole wear is only average. The upper is nylon and suede. It uses U-box lacing, and has a padded ankle and heel collars.
Sizes: 6 to 13
Widths: One standard width

Saucony Trainer 1980. A brand-new shoe for 1978, the Saucony Trainer 1980 has excellent impact qualities and flexibility. It slips somewhat in sole wear—an important consideration. The upper is nylon with suede. It has U-box lacing with padded ankle and heel collars.
Sizes: 6 to 13
Widths: One standard width

Highly Recommended Shoes For Women

Brooks Ladies Vantage. This highly recommended running shoe was introduced in 1978. Its excellent impact protection and very good flexibility make it one of the best women's shoes on the market at a reasonable price. Because of all this, the shoe may be difficult to obtain. It has a built-in arch support but no insole. The upper, made of nylon mesh, features speed lacing, and padded ankle and heel collars.
Sizes: 4 to 10
Widths: One standard width

Brooks Ladies Vantage Supreme. Also introduced in 1978, the Supreme is a very good shoe. But the Brooks Ladies Vantage is a much better buy and a

BROOKS LADIES VANTAGE

marginally better shoe. The Supreme has a spike-like stud tread and a built-in support system. Its upper is nylon with suede trim. It has U-box lacing, and padded ankle and heel collars.
Sizes: 4 to 10
Widths: One standard width

New Balance W320. The W320 was introduced in 1978. Its construction is similar to the 320 for men, and it, too, is an excellent shoe. Fortunately, the toe box is larger than is usual for most New Balance shoes. The W320 is rated highly in impact protection. It has a herringbone tread, two layers under the forefoot 14.5mm thick and three layers under the heel 27mm thick. There is a polyurethane arch support but no insole. The upper is nylon with suede trim. It features padded ankle and heel counters. This is a very good shoe for women with feet of unusual width.
Sizes: 4 to 10
Widths: AA to D

Tiger Tigress. An excellent women's shoe, the Tigress has been around only since 1977. The Tigress has a herringbone tread, two layers under the forefoot, an expanded rubber arch support, and a terry cloth foam insole. The upper is nylon. It has U-box lacing, and padded ankle and heel collars.
Sizes: 3 to 10
Widths: One standard width

Racing Flats

Racing flats are designed for speed. They are lighter in weight than training flats and usually have thinner soles. You need not be a track star before you buy a pair, but you should be a serious runner who races against time (your own or that of others). The beginner is better off with training flats.

Men have a wide variety of racing flats to choose from, but the selection is much more limited for women. This is particularly unfortunate because so many women are getting involved in marathon running. Only a few years ago, however, there were only a few training flats designed for women. In the near future, manufacturers of racing flats may catch up with the demand as well.

Adidas TRX Competition. The TRX was introduced in 1978. It fits in well with all the other Adidas models and is very well made. It is constructed of nylon with suede trim and the color is white and blue. It has good rear foot and forefoot impact qualities. Sole flexibility also appears to be very good.
Sizes: 5 to 15
Widths: One standard width

Converse International. This is another shoe which was just introduced in 1978. It appears to be a very well constructed shoe and has good impact qualities. The shoe also contains a padded Achilles tendon protector.
Sizes: 6 to 13
Widths: One standard width

Converse WC Marathoner. Long known for athletic shoes, Converse entered the racing flat market with this shoe. It is very lightweight and receives top scores for flexibility. The star pattern tread does not provide as much traction as some other models, but is quite durable. Shock absorption is better than aver-

age and the nylon mesh upper offers breathability.
Sizes: 6 to 13
Widths: Narrow, Medium, and Wide

EB Marathon. This leather shoe is rather expensive but the sole durability is excellent and so is the flexibility. The waffle tread provides good traction. This is a well constructed shoe.
Sizes: 3½ to 14
Widths: One standard width

EB Race Walker. This shoe was first introduced in 1972. It is another shoe made of calf leather. It is beige and has padded ankle and heel collars. Although the shoe was made for race walking, many road runners use it for marathon racing as well. It has excellent sole wear and above average flexibility.
Sizes: 3½ to 14
Widths: One standard width

EB Sao Paulo. This is a shoe that has been around since 1972. It is essentially the same shoe that was introduced in 1972. It seems to be a well made shoe but it appears to have only average impact protection for the runner.
Sizes: 3½ to 13
Widths: One standard width

Nike Elite. Last year this was the finest racing flat made. Today it is still an excellent shoe but the competitors are getting close. It has typical good Nike construction and it has pretty good impact qualities. The shoe has the Nike waffle tread design.
Sizes: 3 to 13
Widths: One standard width

Nike Sting. This is a good shoe but it is rapidly being overtaken by the Nike Elite and Waffle Racer. It is a durable shoe that offers excellent shock absorption qualities. Flat tread provides good traction and a wide heel is a definite asset. The nylon-suede upper is rugged.
Sizes: 3 to 13
Widths: One standard width

Nike Waffle Racer. This is the Nike Elite's own competitor. It has better traction and wear. An excellent heel counter. Again, good quality Nike construction. It's a nylon with suede trim and green and black coloring. An excellent buy.
Sizes: 3 to 13
Widths: One standard width

Women's Racing Flats

Adidas Lady TRX Comp. This shoe was first introduced in 1978. It is an excellent shoe made in the fine Adidas tradition. It has a studded tread and the uppers are made of nylon with a suede trim. The color is white and blue. It has average sole wear, good flexibility and very good to excellent rear and forefoot impact qualities. It's one racing flat that can be recommended for women. A good buy.
Sizes: 4 to 11
Widths: One standard width

MANUFACTURERS OF RECOMMENDED SHOES

Adidas USA Inc.
2382 Townsgate Rd.
Westlake Village, CA
91361

Brooks Shoe Mfg. Co.
131 Factory St.
Hanover, PA 17331

Converse Rubber Co.
55 Fordham Rd.
Wilmington, MA 01887

E.B. Sport International
Lydiard Enterprise
Box 180
Basking Ridge, NJ 07920

New Balance Athletic Shoes
38-42 Everett St.
Boston, MA 02134

Nike
8285 S.W. Nimbus Ave.
Beaverton, OR 97005

Saucony
12 Peach St.
Kutztown, PA 19530

Tiger
Asics Sports of America
2052 Alton Ave.
Irvine, CA 92714

Sources

There are many sources that you may want to consider for information and help on marathon running. There are, for example, organizations and publications that provide news about marathons and running in general.

The organizations sponsor events, pass on information, and sometimes offer discounts on equipment. At the very least they provide a sense of community, assuring the runner that a lot of other people are equally interested.

Magazines and newsletters are, quite frankly, the best way to keep up-to-date on what's happening in the world of running and marathoning. Articles cover a wide range of topics of interest to the runner, including dates and places of events, interviews, advice, and helpful hints. Even the ads can be fascinating reading, keeping you informed about all the latest products.

The American runner is doubly fortunate because there are regional publications also.

Organizations Especially For Runners

Amateur Athletic Union (AAU), AAU House, 3400 W. 86th St., Indianapolis, IN 45268.

American Medical Jogger's Association, Box 4704, North Hollywood, CA 91607.

The National Jogging Association (NJA), 919 18th St., N.W., Washington, DC 20006.

National Track and Field Hall of Fame, 1524 Kanawha Blvd., Charleston, WV 25311.

President's Council on Physical Fitness and Sports,

Washington, DC 20201.

Roadrunner's Club of America (RRCA), 1111 Army-Navy Drive, Arlington, VA 22202.

Young Men's Christian Association (YMCA), 291 Broadway, New York, NY 10007.

Major Magazines

The Jogger, National Jogging Association, 919 18th St., N.W., Washington, DC 20006.

The Marathoner, World Publications, Box 366, Mountain View, CA 94042.

On The Run, World Publications, Box 366, Mountain View, CA 94042.

Roadrunner's Club New York Association Newsletter, 226 East 53rd St., New York, NY 10022.

The Runner, One Park Avenue, New York, NY 10016.

Runner's World, World Publications, Box 366, Mountain View, CA 94042.

Running, Box 350, Salem, OR 97308.

Sports Medicine, 4530 W. 77th St., Minneapolis, MN 55435.

Today's Jogger, Stories, Layouts, & Press, Inc., 257 Park Ave., S., New York, NY 10010.

Track and Field News, Box 296, Los Altos, CA 94022.

Local And Regional Magazines

Noc Cal Running Review, PO Box 1551, San Mateo, CA 94401.

Running Times, 1816 Lamont St., N.W., Washington, DC 20010.

Yankee Runner, Box 237, Merrimac, MA 01860.